THE UK
TEDDY BEAR
GUIDE 2018

GW00641034

THE UK
TEDDY BEAR
GUIDE 2018

Further copies
are available from the publisher

WMM Publishing
St James House, 13 Kensington Square, London, W8 5HD

You can order online: www.hugglets.co.uk
Single copies: UK £7.50, Europe £8.50, Rest of World £10.50 inc postage

ISBN 978-1-870880-45-9

Cover Photo: Courtesy of Sandra Kunz

Published by:
WMM Publishing
St James House
13 Kensington Square
London, W8 5HD

Tel: +44 (0)20/77 95 81 33
info@wmmpublishing.co.uk
www.wmmpublishing.co.uk

Printed in Great Britain by Newman Thomson, Burgess Hill, England

The UK Teddy Bear Guide 2018 is compiled and published in October 2017.

Great care has been taken to ensure the accuracy of information given and it is believed to be correct at the time of going to press. However, no liability can be accepted for loss or damage resulting from error or omission of any sort. Information is invited to ensure the future accuracy and comprehensive coverage of the Guide.

Readers are required to satisfy themselves on all matters concerning advertisers' standards, products and services, and no liability will be accepted by WMM Publishing in any way.

Welcome to the Guide

Welcome to the 31st annual edition of the Hugglets UK Teddy Bear Guide

We're delighted to present this fully revised and updated edition of the Guide for 2018. The Guide contains a wealth of valuable information and pictures to help you locate treasures to add to your collection.

We hope you'll be able to make good use of the free Hugglets Festivals tickets in the last few pages of the Guide.

The Winter BearFest and the Teddies Festival 2018 take place at Kensington Town Hall in London and provide rare opportunities to meet so many bear artists in person. As well as seeing (and cuddling) thousands of unique creations from around the world of course.

I If you haven't already done so please do visit www.hugglets.co.uk and register to help us keep in touch about the Festivals and Guide. You can also meet with us at Facebook and Instagram.

When contacting businesses you see in these pages please let them know you saw them in the Hugglets UK Teddy Bear Guide.

We look forward to meeting many of you at the Hugglets Festivals in February and September 2018.

Sebastian Marquardt
WMM Publishing

On our front cover this year we feature a wonderful creation by Sandra Kunz.

Let's keep in touch
www.hugglets.co.uk
www.facebook.com/hugglets
www.instagram.com/hugglets.uk

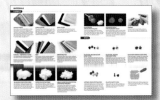
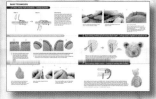

Many of the shops listed here are specialist teddy bear shops, but we also include toy and gift shops which have a range of bears on sale.

Readers are advised to telephone for stock details and opening times before travelling a distance. The Teddy Bear Trail section (page 125) also gives location and stock information.

Some entries are 'mail order only' or dealers to visit by appointment. Some international entries are also included and are indicated by a globe.

- Collectors of old bears should turn to page 16.

- Many bear artists also sell directly - see page 62.

● ABBEY BEARS
11 The Market, Padstow, Cornwall, PL28 8AL
☎ 01841 532484
email: abbeybears@hotmail.co.uk
Please see display advertisement.

● ABRACADABRA TEDDY BEARS
8A Cross Street, Saffron Walden, Essex, CB10 1EX
☎ 01799 527222
email: marsha@abracadabra-teddies.com
web: www.abracadabra-teddies.com
Artist bears our speciality, shop exclusives, top brands, vintage, orphanage, dolls, realistic animals, flexible layaway, mail order worldwide.

ATIQUE & URCHINS BEARS

Steiff

BATH HOUSE FORE STREET
TINTAGEL CORNWALL
01840 779009
www.urchinsbears.com

The Bacton Bears

MANY COLLECTABLES AND GIFT IDEAS
**Over 1000 bears and animals
in stock at any time**
Stockists of Steiff, Deans, Merrythought, Hermann, Deb Canham,
Le bert Leather Goods, Shoebutton Bears, Jellycat and Puppet Company

Steiff DEAN'S

Open Mon-Fri , 9am - 5-30pm and Saturday 9am-5pm
Station Garage, Broad Road,
Bacton, Stowmarket, IP14 4HP
T: 01449 781087 E: bactonbears@aol.com
www.bactonbears.co.uk

● ASHBY BEARS

5 Stephenson Court, Brindley Road, Coalville,
Leicestershire, LE67 3HG
☎ 01530 564444
email: sales@ashbybears.com
web: www.ashbybears.com
East Midlands largest selection since 2001. Club store
for most leading manufacturers. Purchase securely on
our hugely popular web site www.ashbybears.com

● ASQUITHS WORLD FAMOUS TEDDY BEAR SHOP

2-4 New Street, Henley-on-Thames, Oxon, RG9 2BT
☎ 01491 571978
email: sales@asquiths.com
web: www.asquiths.com
Large stocks of Charlie Bears, Isabelle Bears, Asquiths
English Bears, Steiff, HM Bears, Hermann and Hansa
friends. 30 seconds from the Thames.

● ATIQUE & URCHINS BEARS

Bath House, Fore Street, Tintagel, Cornwall, PL34 0DA
☎ 01840 779009
email: sales@urchinsbears.com
web: www.urchinsbears.com
Contemporary & Antique Steiff Bears, Charlie & Isabelle
Bears, Kaycee Bears, Merrythought, Canterbury Bears,
Deb Canham, many unique artist bears. Open all year!

● BACTON BEARS

at Jeffries, Station Garage, Bacton, Stowmarket,
Suffolk, IP14 4HP
☎ 01449 781087
email: bactonbears@aol.com
web: www.bactonbears.co.uk
Literally hundreds of bears! Steiff Club Store.
Merrythought, Hermann, Dean's, Leebert, Shoebutton
Bears, Jellycat and many more. Visit our website!

● BAKEWELL GIFT & BEAR SHOP

8 Matlock St, Bakewell, Derbyshire, DE45 1EE
☎ 01629 814811
email: info@giftsandbears.co.uk
web: www.giftsandbears.co.uk
Collector / plush bears including Steiff, Charlie Bears,
Jellycat, Gund. Also giftware, Beatrix Potter, baby gifts.
Plus mail order and internet.

BEAR ESSENTIALS

Silver Bear Centre, Anke Morgenroth, Bawnboy,
County Cavan, Ireland
☎ +353 (0)49 9523461 mob: +353 (0)87 7610537
email: info@bearessentials.ie
web: www.bearessentials.ie or www.facebook.
com/Bearessentials.ie
Online stockist of Charlie Bears, Steiff, own L.E. Irish
bears & baby gifts. T.B. Hospital, visitor centre, workshops & events.

BEAR GALLERY

5 Loan Rd, Cullybackey, County Antrim BT42 1ER
☎ 028 2588 2262
email: sales@beargallery.co.uk
web: www.beargallery.uk.com
We specialise in Steiff Bears and animals. Also stockists
of Hermann, Clemens, Artist Bears and other leading
brands. Callers by appointment only.

THE BEAR GARDEN

10 Jeffries Passage, Guildford, Surrey, GU1 4AP
☎ 01483 302581
email: bears@beargarden.co.uk
web: www.beargarden.co.uk
Established 1992. Leading UK teddy bear specialist. Ex-
perts in Steiff, Charlie, Merrythought, 'both' Hermanns,
Clemens, Kösen, artist bears and more!

THE BEAR NECESSITIES

Groeninge 23, 8000 Brugge, Belgium
☎ +32 (0)5034 1027 Fax: As tel.
web: www.thebearnecessities.be
Steiff Club store set in the heart of beautiful Brugge.
Home of Knarf handmade artist bears and many more.

THE BEAR SHOP

18 Elm Hill, Norwich, Norfolk, NR3 1HN
☎ 01603 766866
email: enquiries@bearshops.co.uk
web: www.bearshops.co.uk
Exclusive Teddy Bear Shop in Norwich. Top artists and
leading manufacturers. New Bears always arriving. Open
Mon-Sat 10am-5pm, Sun 11am-4pm.

BEARS ON THE SQUARE

2 The Square, Ironbridge, Shropshire, TF8 7AQ
☎ 01952 433924 Fax: 01952 433926
email: teddies@bearsonthesquare.com
web: www.bearsonthesquare.com
**The Midland's largest selection of bears from
major manufacturers and leading artists. Many
shop exclusives. Worldwide mail order service.**

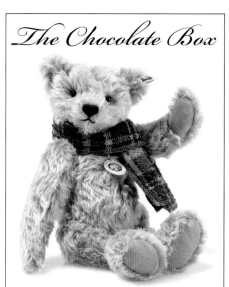

The Chocolate Box

Limited edition bears for collectors.
Steiff, Charlie Bears, Kaycee, Merrythought.
Open Tues to Sat 10-5pm, Sun 11-4pm. ☎ 01484 688222

www.chocolateandbears.com

When contacting advertisers

please mention you saw their advertisement in the

UK Teddy Bear Guide 2018

● BEARS TO COLLECT

Tilbrook Mill, B645, Lower Dean, Nr Kimbolton,
Huntingdon, Cambridgeshire, PE28 0LH
☎ 01480 860376
email: shirley@bears2collect.co.uk
web: www.bears2collect.co.uk
Specialists in limited edition and collectable bears
including Steiff, Charlie Bears, Deb Canham, Teddy
Hermann, artist bears and more.

● BREWINS' BRUINS

The Swanage Teddy Bear Shop, 5 Mermond Place,
Swanage, Dorset, BH19 1DG
☎ 01929 761398 (call for opening times)
email: lube@brewinsbruins.co.uk
web: www.brewinsbruins.co.uk
Enjoy a day in Swanage and visit our bear shop - home
and sponsors of the ITBAA International Teddy Bear
Artists' Awards.

● CEJAIS BEARS & DOLLSHOUSES

169 Medieval Spon Street, Coventry, Warwickshire,
CV1 3BB
☎ 024 76 633630
email: collect@cejais.net
web: www.cejais.net
Charlie Bears, Steiff, Isabelle, Dean's, Gund, Cotswold,
Merrythought, Kaycee, Paddington, Heartfelt, Aurora,
Canterbury Bears, Clemens, Silver Tag Bears.

● THE CHOCOLATE BOX

Hollowgate, Holmfirth, West Yorkshire, HD9 2DG
☎ 01484 688222
email: gillian.marshall@tiscali.co.uk
web: www.chocolateandbears.com
Limited edition bears for collectors. Steiff, Charlie Bears,
Kaycee, Merrythought. .Open Tues to Sat 10.00 to
5.00pm, Sun 11-4pm

● CORFE BEARS

Hayley and Stacey Maskell, 37 High Street,
Swanage, Dorset, BH19 2LT
☎ 01929 426827
email: enq@corfebears.co.uk
web: www.corfebears.co.uk
Steiff Club Store, Charlie Bears, Kaycee, most manufacturers, various artists. Postage FOC. Open 7 days 10-5.
Friendly, reliable service - try us!!

● EARTH ANGELS STUDIOS

Jen O'Connor, Warwick, New York, USA
☎ +1 845 986 8720
email: jen@EarthAngelsStudios.com
web: www.EarthAngelsStudios.com

Since 1996, we've presented talented bear, heirloom toy, soft sculpture and folk artists on our gallery-style website and at events.

● FUZZIES FLUFF N STUFF

Gina Foster
☎ 01706 372562 option 4
email: sales@fuzziesfluffnstuff.co.uk
web: www.fuzziesfluffnstuff.co.uk

We sell collectables and gifts for all occasions, including Charlie Bears! Check out our website.

● HANSA CREATION INC.

Action Agents Limited, 1 Georgian Close, Stanmore, Middlesex, HA7 3QT
Tel: 020 8954 5956
email: info@hansa-uk.com
web: www.hansa-uk.com

WORLD-RENOWNED COLLECTION OF AMAZINGLY LIFE-LIKE (AND LIFE-SIZE), HAND-CRAFTED PLUSH ANIMALS.

● KIERON JAMES TOYS

79 High Street, Lindfield, West Sussex, RH16 2HN
☎ 01444 484870
email: kieron.info@yahoo.co.uk
web: www.kieronjamestoys.co.uk

A shop in picturesque Lindfield village for fine teddy bears and gifts. Steiff, Hermann, Charlie Bears and Jellycat etc. Credit, debit cards accepted.

● KINGSWEAR BEARS AND FRIENDS

2A The Square, Kingswear, Dartmouth, Devon, TQ6 0AA
☎ 01803 752632
email: teddies@kingswearbears.com
web: www.kingswearbears.com

Riverside shop near Dartmouth, opposite the Steam Railway from Torbay. Packed full of bears including Charlie Bears.

● KOKO'S BEAR SHOP

16 Union Street, Ryde, Isle of Wight, PO33 2DU
☎ 01983 616815
email: sales@kokosbearshop.com
web: www.kokosbearshop.com

Extensive range from affordable cuddlies to unique hand-made artist collections and limited edition miniatures! Buy online. Flexible layaway service available.

● MAGPIES GIFTS LTD

Unit 4 Trago Mills, Newton Abbot, Devon, TQ12 6JD
☎ 01626 353456 mob: 07777 681123
email: sales@magpies-gifts.co.uk
web: www.charliebearsuk.com and
www.magpies-gifts.co.uk

Located at the out of town shopping centre, 'Trago Mills' stocking Charlie Bears, Steiff, Kaycee, Artist Bears and much more!

● MUMBLES

Katie Stewart, 13 Shairps Business Park, Livingston, EH54 5FD
☎ 01506 437226
email: marketing@henbury.com
web: www.the-mumbles.co.uk

Soft, cuddly, adorable - the Mumbles collection has a range of promotional bears, animals and accessories to suit all brands and events.

● PAWS IN THE FOREST

27 High Street, Lyndhurst, Hampshire, SO43 7BE
☎ 02380 282697
email: maggieparma@hotmail.co.uk
Collectables and bears by Steiff, Hermann, Charlie, Deb Canham, Hardy Bears, Kaycee Bears, Isabelle Collection, Hansa and much more.

● SERENDIPITY

1 The Old Bank, 2 Silver Street, Halifax, HX1 1HS
☎ 01422 340097
email: sales@tedshop.com
web: www.tedshop.com
Stockist of Steiff, Dean's, Charlie, Merrythought, Kaycee and others. Also dolls and accessories, dolls houses and twelfth scale miniatures.

● MARY SHORTLE

9 Lord Mayors Walk, York, North Yorkshire, YO31 7HB also at 9, 17 Queen's Arcade, Leeds, LS1 6LF
☎ 01132 456160 / 452 005 York: 01904 631165
email: maryshortle@btopenworld.com
web: www.maryshortle.com
Antique and modern teddies. Limited editions, miniature teddies, leading artists. Teddy bear hospital. Hundreds of teddies to choose from.

● SMIFFY BEARS

74 Cobblestone Walk, High Street, Steyning, West Sussex, BN44 3RD
☎ mob: 07885 075890
email: j.smith157@ntlworld.com
web: www.smiffybears.co.uk

A shop where bears are restored by Smiffy. We stock, Charlie Bears, Hermann, Merrythought, Silver Tag bears and vintage bears.

● ST MARTIN'S GALLERY

The Old Church, Mockbeggar Lane, Ibsley, Hampshire, BH24 3PP
☎ 01425 489090 mob: 07711 912277
email: bluebells70@hotmail.com
web: www.stmartinsgallery.co.uk and www. facebook.com/StMartin'sGallery

Charlie Bears, Tailored Teddies, Steiner, Silver Tag and many more in lovely 17th century church setting. Open Thurs-Sun 11-5.

● STONEBOW BEARS

25 Guildhall Street, Lincoln, Lincolnshire, LN1 1TR
☎ 01522 529219
email: info@stonebowbears.co.uk
web: www.stonebowbears.co.uk

Set in the heart of picturesque Cathedral City of Lincoln. Stockist of Steiff, Charlie Bears, Merrythought, Kosen, Kaycee and Artist Bears!

● TEDDY BEAR ATTIC UK

Sharron O'Gorman, The Olde Shoppe, Ewyas Harold, Herefordshire, HR2 0ES, United Kingdom
☎ 01981 241062
email: teddybearattic@theukgiftdirectory.co.uk
web: www.teddybearattic.co.uk

Online and mail order only. New bears and also preloved collectable bears from private collections looking for a new hug to join

● THE TEDDY BEAR MUSEUM SHOP

The Teddy Bear Museum, Corner of High East St & Salisbury St, Dorchester, Dorset, DT1 1JU
☎ 01305 266040
email: info@teddybearmuseum.co.uk
web: www.teddybearmuseum.co.uk

Good selection of teddy bears from a variety of makes to delight all tastes, including collectors› bears and modern collectables.

Let's keep in touch

www.facebook.com/hugglets

● TEDDY BEARS OF WITNEY

99 High Street, Witney, Oxfordshire, OX28 6HY
☎ 01993 706616 Fax: 01993 702344
email: alfonzo@witneybears.co.uk
web: www.teddybears.co.uk

Open 7 days a week. 2018 catalogue (£5) features over 300 teddy bears, mostly limited editions exclusive to us.

● TEDDY BEARS' PICKNICK

PO Box 333, 3960 BH Wijk bij Duurstede, The Netherlands
☎ +31 (0)343 577068
email: picknick@xs4all.nl
web: www.teddybearspicknick.com

Visit our website to see Steiff, Kösen and Artist Bears and Cats, a.o. Forget me not bears. Worldwide mailorder.

● TEDDY BOUTIQUE

5 Mill Bridge, Skipton, BD23 1NJ
☎ 01756 709676 mob: 07504 163127
email: sales@teddyboutique.com
web: www.teddyboutique.com

Skipton's stunning selection of bears, dolls and gifts, for all ages and occasions. Also available at www.teddyboutique.com and www.facebook.com/TeddyBoutiqueUK

● TEDDY STATION

Victoria Shopping Centre, Southend, Essex, SS2 5SP
☎ 01702 611106
email: teddystation@btinternet.com
web: www.teddystation.co.uk

Southend's specialist shop for Steiff, Charlie Bears, Deb Canham, Hermann and Merrythought. Largest Steiff stockist in Essex. Official Steiff Club shop.

● TIN SOLDIERS STUDIO

PO Box 61095, Pierre van Reyneveld 0045, Pretoria, South Africa
☎ +27 (0)83 305 5954
email: megan@tinsoldiers.co.za
web: www.tinsoldiers.co.za

Artist bears, dolls, gollies, animals and dolls house miniatures for sale. Kits and patterns, toy making supplies.

● TREASURED TEDDIES

at Farnborough Garden Centre, Southam Road, Farnborough, Banbury, Oxfordshire, OX17 1EL
☎ 01295 690479
web: farnboroughgardencentre.co.uk/teddies.html

The teddy lover's garden centre. Treasured gifts for every occasion. Cuddly collectables and furry friends.

● UNA CASA & CO

2-6-18-205 Shinsenrihigashimachi, Toyonaka, Osaka, 560-0082, Japan
☎ +81 (0)6 6170 6579 Fax: As tel.
email: unacasa@unacasa.co.jp
web: www.unacasa.co.jp

Specializing in finest Japanese artist bears including Saeri Omachi and Yuko Nakayama. Worldwide shipping. Please visit our website.

● WORKS OF HEART

1643 Fieldbrook St., Henderson, NV, 89052, USA
☎ +1 702 448 9519
email: bonniesbears@yahoo.com
web: www.bonniesbearshop.com

I stock a large inventory of Charlie Bears, Kaycee Bears and artist bears. I ship worldwide. Visit my website or while visiting Vegas.

END

Welcome to this section on sources for old bears. Many are dealers who operate on an appointment basis or sell through fairs and the internet. Some have shops, and auction houses and museums are also included.

The numbers of old bears held in stock may range from under ten to over 100. Readers are advised to telephone regarding stock and viewing arrangements before travelling a distance.

● BEARS AT THE VALE
Kimberley Burns, 177B Lanark Road, Maida Vale, London, W9 1NX
☎ 0207 328 2280 mob: 07493 681592
email: info@bearsatthevale.com
web: www.bearsatthevale.com
London specialists in a wide variety Antique, Vintage and Artist Bears and collectables.

● BEBES ET JOUETS
☎ 01289 304802
email: bebesetjouets@tiscali.co.uk
Finest antique teddies and dolls. Large selection. Genuine old bears, no repros. Photos available. Email or telephone for friendly assistance.

● BEBESANDBRUINS.COM
email: bebesandbruins@yahoo.com
web: www.bebesandbruins.com
A website specialising in antique teddy bears, dolls & their clothing, accessories & related items. Shipping worldwide for 25 years.

● BLAKESLEY BEARS LTD
☎ 01865 600587 mob: 07752 128992
email: lizzie@blakesleybears.com
web: www.blakesleybears.com
Beautiful vintage bears and soft toys bought and sold. Find us online and at Towcester Antiques Market on Fridays.

● BOURTON BEARS
☎ 01452 700608 Fax: As tel.
email: help@bourtonbears.com
web: www.bourtonbears.com
Antique teddy bears - over 350 in stock from Steiff, Chiltern, Farnell, Schuco, Bing, Merrythought and more. We also buy teddies.

● BREWINS' BRUINS
The Swanage Teddy Bear Shop, 5 Mermond Place, Swanage, Dorset, BH19 1DG
☎ 01929 761398 (call for opening times)
email: lube@brewinsbruins.co.uk
web: www.brewinsbruins.co.uk
Enjoy a day in Swanage and visit our bear shop - vintage bears and restoration undertaken. Valuations.

THE BRITISH BEAR COLLECTION

Banwell Castle, Banwell, Somerset, BS29 6NX
☎ 01934 822263/822342
email: c_parsons@hotmail.co.uk
web: www.thebritishbearcollection.co.uk
A unique collection of British teddy bears. Not currently on public display. Enquiries welcome.

BRITISH TEDDY BEAR FESTIVAL AT WOBURN ABBEY

☎ mob: 07875 874854
email: hap@mkps.co.uk
web: www.115yearsofteddybears.com
Sunday 10th June 2018 10am-4pm

C&T AUCTIONS

Unit 4, High House Business Park, Kenardington, Ashford, Kent, TN26 2LF
☎ mob: 07736 668702
email: leigh.gotch@candtauctions.co.uk
web: www.candtauctions.co.uk
For enquiries concerning buying and selling at C&T Auctions please contact Leigh Gotch.

DOLLS, BEARS AND BYGONES

☎ 07889 630051
email: dollsbearsbygone@aol.com
web: www.dollsbearsandbygones.co.uk
Wide selection of gorgeous old bears, fine quality antique dolls and accessories. Worldwide shipping. Visit my website to see!

MORPHEUS WILSON

Elaine Wilson, Cumbria
☎ mob: 07548 120977
email: Morpheuswilson1@gmail.com
web: www.facebook.com/MorpheusWilsonVintage
www.instagram.com/Morpheuswilson
Old teddies & vintage soft toys including cats & dogs.

THE OLD BEAR COMPANY

☎ 01246 850117
email: oldbears@oldbear.co.uk
web: www.oldbearcompany.com
Old teddy bears - please visit our website which is regularly updated! www.oldbearcompany.com

OLD BEARS LODGE

☎ 01443 776031
email: info@oldbearslodge.co.uk
web: www.oldbearslodge.co.uk
At Old Bears Lodge you will find a selection of old and cherished bears from your childhood days.

OLD BEARS NETWORK

Brown Cow Cottage, Godly Lane, Rishworth, Sowerby Bridge, West Yorkshire, HX6 4QR
☎ 01422 823079
email: oldbears.network@zen.co.uk
web: www.oldbearsnetwork.com
Vintage and antique teddy bears from around the world, plus clothing and accessories. We update regularly!

OLD TEDDY BEAR SHOP

☎ 01404 823444
email: mail@oldteddybearshop.co.uk
web: www.oldteddybearshop.co.uk
Antique, old & very special Steiff teddy bears and old teddy bears from around the world. Worldwide shipping.

● ONCE UPON A TIME BEARS

29 Northfield Road, Wetwang, East Yorkshire,
YO25 9XY
☎ 01377 236621 mob: 07527 457398
email: onceuponatimebears@yahoo.co.uk
web: www.onceuponatimebears.co.uk
A lovely selection always of vintage and antique bears,
animals and beautiful clothing and accessories for all
your bears.

● THE OPTIMISTS

☎ 07769 157406
email: gill@theoptimists.net
web: www.rubylane.com/shops/theoptimists
**Vintage bears, dolls and soft toys. Norah Wellings
specialist.**

● SUE PEARSON

at Emporium Antiques Centre, Cliffe High St, Lewes,
East Sussex
☎ 01273 595734
email: sales@suepearson.co.uk
web: www.suepearson.co.uk
Probably the finest selection of vintage bears available.
Sue is available by appointment.

● SPECIAL AUCTION SERVICES

☎ 01635 580595 mob: 0751 500 4635
email: daniel@specialauctionservices.com
web: www.specialauctionservices.com
A bi-annual auction of teddy bears and dolls organised by Daniel Agnew, held in Newbury, Berkshire.

● SPIELZEUG WELTEN MUSEUM BASEL

Toy Worlds Museum Basle, Steinenvorstadt 1,
Basel, CH-4051, Switzerland
☎ +41 (0)61 225 95 95 Fax: +41 (0)61 225 95 96
web: www.swmb.museum
The collection is the only one of its kind in Europe. Home
of the world's largest collection of old teddy bears.

● SUNNY VINTAGE & RETRO AND TEDDY HOSPITAL

262 Northdown Road, Cliftonville, Kent, CT9 2PX
☎ mob: 07426 251117
email: theteddymaster@gmail.com
web: www.bbears.co.uk
Vintage & Retro shop, mid-century furniture, lighting,
toys, antique dolls and bears, vintage fabrics, original
art. Teddy hospital. Free valuations.

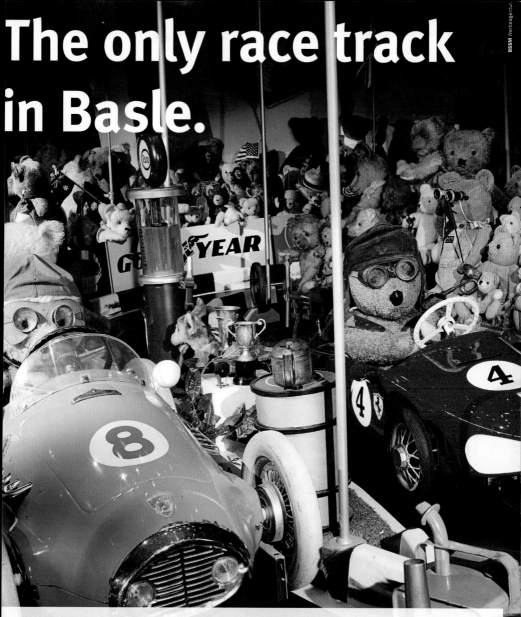

The only race track in Basle.

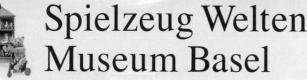

Spielzeug Welten Museum Basel

Toy Worlds Museum Basle | Museum, Tuesday to Sunday from 10 to 18, in December, daily from 10 to 18 | Ristorante La Sosta and Boutique, daily from 9.30 to 18
Steinenvorstadt 1, CH-4051 Basel | www.swmb.museum

TEDDY BEAR ATTIC UK

Sharron O'Gorman, The Olde Shoppe, Ewyas Harold,
Herefordshire, HR2 0ES, United Kingdom
☎ 01981 241062
email: teddybearattic@theukgiftdirectory.co.uk
web: www.teddybearattic.co.uk

Online and mail order only. New bears and also
preloved collectable bears from private collections
looking for a new hug to join.

TEDDY BEAR MUSEUM

Hilary Pauley, Grandma's Teddies
email: hap@mkps.co.uk
web: www.teddybear-museum.co.uk

The teddybear-museum is a pictorial record of old
bears to help collectors to identify the make, type and
date of their bears.

V&A MUSEUM OF CHILDHOOD

Cambridge Heath Road, London, E2 9PA
☎ 020 898 35200
email: moc@vam.ac.uk
web: www.museumofchildhood.org.uk

The museum has a collection of over 400 bears with
about 75 on display.

VECTIS AUCTIONS

Fleck Way, Thornaby, Stockton-on-Tees, Cleveland,
TS17 9JZ
☎ 01642 750616 Fax: 01642 769478
email: admin@vectis.co.uk
web: www.vectis.co.uk

The largest toy auctioneer in the world.

END

FESTIVALS

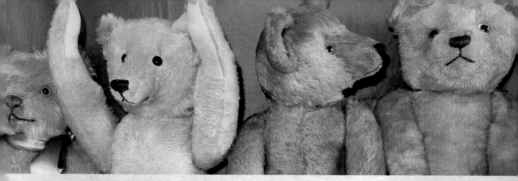

Teddy bears from 1900 to 1950's

Search for your own teddy bear!

Teddy bears with no identification mark or label are classed as "similar to"

We would love to showcase your bears so that others can see them.

We have some lovely visitors already!

Tel: 07875874854

Email: hap@mkps.co.uk

http://www.teddybear-museum.co.uk

Oldest British Bear Companies

Drawing on the research so far in our 10,000 Bear Maker Project we've compiled this provisional index of British bear manufacturers operating prior to 1970. Over the years some companies were taken over by others which makes the tracking of dates quite difficult. No doubt some of these dates will be revised. It's also possible that some of these companies were marketing bears made elsewhere. Although we think these companies were making teddy bears prior to 1970 some of them were not making bears when their company first started.

The history of British bears is an evolving subject so if you are keen on this topic please post your findings and pictures on the Hugglets website.

Business and brand names	Started (approx)
Alresford Crafts Ltd	1970
Aneeta	1930
Atlas Manufacturing Company	1915
B.G. Toys Ltd	1963
Thomas Baxter	1915
Be-Be Dolls Ltd, also Blossom Toys, Carousel, Blue Ribbon Playthings	1941
Bell & Bell	1959
Benson's Cuddly Toys	1938
Blue Ribbon Toy Company	1950
Britannia Toy Company Ltd, also Britannia Toys Works	1915
British United Toy Manufacturing Co, also Omega	1894
J. & A.J. Burman Ltd, also Zoo Toy Company, Fondle Toys	1919
Chad Valley Co Ltd, also Aerolite, Magna	1919
Channel Island Toys	1966
Chiltern, also H.G. Stone & Co, Leon Rees, Hugme	1908
Dandycraft Toys	1950
Dean's Rag Book Company Ltd, also Dean's Childsplay Toys Ltd, Dean's Rag Book Co (1903) Ltd, Gwentoys	1903
Ealon Toys, also East London Federation Toy Factory	1939
East Sussex Toys	1917
J.K. Farnell, also Alpha Toys, Alphalyte, Silkalite	1904
Gottschalk & Davis	1915
Gray & Nicholls	1920

Gross & Schild	1925
Gwentoys Ltd	1934
H M Bears, also HM Toys, Lakeland Toys, Rowland & Iris Chesney	1969
Harwin & Co Ltd	1914
Hawksley & Co	1915
House of Nisbet, also Bully Bears	1953
Invicta	1935
Isaacs & Company, also Isa Toys	1915
W. H. Jones, also William Henry Jones	1914
H. J. Julian	1915
Jumbo Toys - A. Young & Sons	1915
Jungle Toys	1932
Keel Toys Ltd, also Keeltoys UK	1947
Lefray Toys Ltd	1948
Merrythought Ltd, also W.G. Holmes, G.H. Laxton, Cheeky, Merrythought Toys Ltd	1930
Minibrix Hygienic Toys	1959
Naomi Laight	1970
S. Oppenheimer, Ltd., also Emu	1950
Peacock & Company, also W. Peacock Brothers, Peacocks, Peacock Bros	1853
Pedigree Toys, also Lines Bros, Lines Brothers	1931
Pixie Toys	1930
Ralf Dunn and Company	1909
S & L Manufacturing Co. Ltd	1932
South Wales Toy Co Ltd, also Madingland	1917
Star Manufacturing Company, also Swan Toys	1916
Steevans Manufacturing Co	1908
The Teddy Toy Company, also TTC, A Simmonds, Softanlite	1918
Terryer Toys, also Ahso-light	1890
Tinka Bell, also Plummer Wandless (Wholesale) Ltd	1946
Twyford, also Acton Toycraft Ltd	1968
Nora Wellings, also Victoria Toy Works	1935
Wendy Boston, also Playsafe, Wendy Boston Playsafe Toys Ltd	1945
The Wholesale Toy Company	1917
Worthing Toy Factory Ltd	1922

END

Teddy Bear Fairs and Organisers

A list of the fair dates known at the time of publication can be found in the Fair Dates listing on page 30.

Dates can change so we recommend you confirm details with organisers before travelling a distance.

● ALTON TEDDY BEAR FESTIVAL

Alton Assembly Rooms, High Street, Hampshire GU34 1BA

☎ 07738 092768

email: altonteddybearfestival@hotmail.com

For all bear enthusiasts, with collectables, artist bears, OOAK, bear making supplies, clothes, furniture & pre-loved bears

● ART DOLL EXPO

(Shanghai Uideal Creative Design Service Co., Ltd.), Amelia Wang, Room 434, Central Plaza, Huaqiao International Service Business Park, Kunshan, Jiangsu Province, 215332, China

☎ mob: +86 136 019 20831

email: artdollexpo@hotmail.com

web: www.artdoll-expo.com / VK: ART DOLL EXPO / WeChat: artdollexpo

Organizer of ART DOLL EXPO in China, focusing on market development and cultural communication of doll, bear & small sculpture art.

● BREWINS' BRUINS

5 Mermond Place, Swanage, Dorset, BH19 1DG

☎ 01929 761398 (call for opening times)

email: lube@brewinsbruins.co.uk

web: www.brewinsbruins.co.uk

Organisers: Hampshire Teddy Bear Festivals and ITBAA International Teddy Bear Artists' Awards. Venue: Lyndhurst Community Centre SO43 7NY (See Fair Dates).

Doll and Teddy Fairs

At The National Motorcycle Museum, Birmingham

Bickenhill, Nr Birmingham, West Midlands (opposite N.E.C. Junction 6 M42) B92 0EJ

SUNDAY 25TH MARCH 2018
SUNDAY 23RD SEPTEMBER 2018

OPEN 10.30 to 4.00pm

Up to 90 quality stands with antique, collectable, artist and reborn dolls. Old and new teddies and related accessories. Doll & Bear Supplies.

Free Parking • Refreshments • Well Signposted Repair Advice • Free Valuations

Admission £4.00 (Accompanied children FREE)

For further information contact the organiser Debbie Woodhouse (Doll & Teddy Fairs) on 07973 760881
www.dollandteddyfairs.co.uk

The Pudsey Doll & Teddy Fair

At Pudsey Civic Hall, Leeds

SATURDAY 14TH APRIL 2018
SATURDAY 6TH OCTOBER 2018

Dawsons Corner, Stanningley, Pudsey, West Yorkshire LS28 5TA (off the main Leeds Ring Road - A6110)

Open 10.30 to 4.00

Up to 84 quality stands with antique, collectable, artist, reproduction and reborn dolls. Old and new teddies and related juvenalia. Plus mohair and bear making supplies, dolls kits and accessories.

Free Parking • Refreshments • Well Signposted Repair Advice • Free Valuations

Admission £3.50 (Accompanied children 50p)

For further information contact the organiser Debbie Woodhouse Doll & Teddy Fairs on 07973 760881
www.dollandteddyfairs.co.uk

The 26th Japan Teddy Bear with Friends Convention
by Japan Teddy Bear Association

The Biggest Teddy Bear Show in Asia
Inviting All Teddy Bear Fans, Artists & Dealers!

When : July 7 (Sat) - 8 (Sun), 2018

Where : Bellesalle Takadanobaba

3-8-2 Okubo, Shinjuku, Tokyo 169-0072 JAPAN
www.bellesalle.co.jp/shisetsu/shinjuku/bs_takadanobaba

Charity Events and Much More!

Show & Sale

International Teddy Bear & Animal Contest

Show & Sale

Contact: Kayoko Jennings
JTBA Overseas Coordinator   Kayoko.jennings@gmail.com

PREMIER TEDDY BEAR EVENTS

SHEFFIELD
The Great Yorkshire Teddy Bear Event
Sunday 19th November 2017
Sheffield Hilton Hotel
Victoria Quays, S4 7YB
10:30am to 3:00pm

NEW for 2018
STRATFORD
The Great Stratford Teddy Bear Event
Sunday 8th July 2018
Stratford ArtHouse
14 Rother Street, CV37 6LU
10:30am to 3:00pm

Check our website for details
www.thegreatyorkshireteddybearevent.co.uk

www.hantsevents.co.uk

Locks Heath
Teddy Bear Fair

Saturday 11am
21st April till
2018 4pm

Main Hall, Lockswood Community Centre,
Southampton, Hampshire, SO31 6DX

Wonderful Vintage, Antique & New Artists
Teddy Bears as well as fantastic related
Accessories for sale at the Teddy Bear Fair!

Free Parking * Refreshments * Entry Only £1

For Details Call 07841 660177 or email hantsevents@yahoo.co.uk

BRIGHT STAR TEDDY BEAR SHOWS ONLINE
3428 Hillvale Road, Louisville, KY, 40241, USA
☎ +1 502 423 7827 mob: +1 502 548 2403 Fax: As tel.
email: brtstar1@aol.com
web: www.bright-star-promotions.com
Sponsors of artist teddy bear shows online and live, in-person shows in several major USA cities.

CORNWALL BEAR FAIRS
Organised by ATIQUE & URCHINS BEARS
☎ 01840 779009
email: sales@urchinsbears.com
web: www.urchinsbears.com
Cornwall Summer 2018 Teddy Bear Festival Sunday 1st July 2018. King Arthurs Great Halls of Chivalry, Fore Street, Tintagel Cornwall PL34 0DA

DOLL & TEDDY FAIRS
Events held at the National Motorcycle Museum and Pudsey Civic Hall
☎ mob: 07973 760881
email: debbie@woodhouse2364.fsnet.co.uk
web: www.dollandteddyfairs.co.uk
Quality fairs with old, collectable, artist bears and dolls. See display advertisements.

DOLLY'S DAYDREAMS
49 High Road, Wisbech, Cambridgeshire, PE13 4ND
☎ 01945 870160 mob: 07860 517048
email: dollysdaydreams@btinternet.com
web: www.dollysdaydreams.com / www.facebook.com/dollysdaydreams
Organisers of events at Newark Showground, Nottinghamshire, featuring Teddies, Dolls & Dolls Houses.

THE GREAT TEDDY BEAR EVENTS COMPANY
Organiser Katherine Hallam
☎ 07852 937518
email: info@katieraebears.co.uk
web: www.thegreatyorkshireteddybearevent.co.uk
Premier Teddy Bear Events in Sheffield and our NEW Stratford Show for 2018. Top teddy bear artists from the UK and overseas.

Woburn Abbey
Teddy Bear Festival

Artist Bears,
Antique and Vintage Bears
and Animals

Sunday 10th
June 2018

10am to
4pm

To book a stand: Tel: 07875874854
Email: hap@mkps.co.uk
www.115yearsofteddybears.com

● LONDON INTERNATIONAL ANTIQUE DOLL, TEDDY BEAR AND TOY FAIR

Kensington Town Hall, Hornton Street, Pillar Hall
Olympia - in 2016
☎ mob: 07875 874854
email: hap@mkps.co.uk
web: www.200yearsofchildhood.com

Sunday 19th November. Fair 10am-4pm. Antique and Vintage. Celebrating 200 years of childhood. 1750s-1950s. Stand enquiries welcome.

● TEDDYBÄR TOTAL

Wellhausen & Marquardt Medien,
Hans-Henny-Jahnn-Weg 51, Hamburg, 22085,
Germany
☎ +49 (0)404291 77100 Fax: +49 (0)404291 77199
email: info@teddybaer-total.com
web: www.teddybaer-total.com

TEDDYBÄR TOTAL is the most international Teddy show with more than 300 artists from more than 25 different nations.

● THE TEDDY BEAR MUSEUM

Corner of High East St & Salisbury St, Dorchester,
Dorset, DT1 1JU
☎ 01305 266040
email: info@teddybearmuseum.co.uk
web: www.teddybearmuseum.co.uk

See Edward Bear and his family of people-sized bears, with teddies from throughout the last century in this enchanting museum.

● BRITISH TEDDY BEAR FESTIVAL AT WOBURN ABBEY

☎ mob: 07875 874854
email: hap@mkps.co.uk
web: www.115yearsofteddybears.com

Join us at Woburn Abbey on Sunday 10th June 2018, from 10am to 4pm, for a day dedicated to teddy bears!

END

Planning Ahead

Dates for your diary:

Sunday	25th	February	2018
Sunday	24th	February	2019
Sunday	23rd	February	2020
Sunday	28th	February	2021

Sunday	9th	September	2018
Sunday	8th	September	2019
Sunday	13th	September	2020
Sunday	12th	September	2021

For exhibitor lists and lots of useful information:
www.hugglets.co.uk

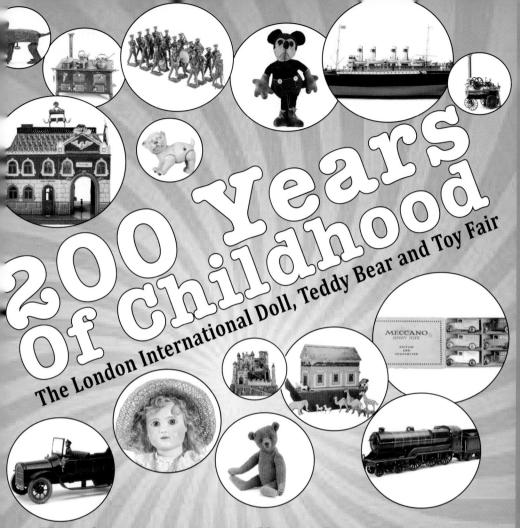

200 Years of Childhood

The London International Doll, Teddy Bear and Toy Fair

Kensington Town Hall London W8 7NX

Sunday 18th November 2018

A dated lined fair, nothing post 1970, the best of antique and vintage toys, diecast, trains, soldiers and figures, games, wooden toys, dolls, dolls' houses and teddy bears.

Organised by Daniel Agnew and Hilary Pauley

Tel: 07875874854 Email: hap@mkps.co.uk

www.200yearsofchildhood.com

Please note that some of these events are not exclusively for bears.

The list has been compiled from information supplied by the organisers who advertise in the Guide. The figure given after the venue specifies, where known, the approximate number of stands, but at non-exclusive shows these are not all teddy bears. Dates and venues can change, so we recommend you confirm details with the organisers before travelling a distance.

October 2017

Sat 28th	Pudsey Doll & Teddy Fair	Pudsey Civic Hall, Pudsey, Leeds, LS28 5TA	10.30am - 4pm	Up to 84	Doll & Teddy Fairs ☎ 07973 760881
Sun 29th	Newark Showground Event	Cedric Ford Pavilion, Newark Showground, NG24 2NY	10.30am - 4pm	90+	Dolly's Daydreams ☎ 01945 870160

November 2017

Sun 5th	Taiwan Teddy Bear Show	Syntrend Creative Park, Taipei	10am - 5pm	40	Taiwan Teddy Bear Association
Sun 5th	Scottish Bear Fair	Troon Concert Hall, Academy Street, Troon, Ayrshire, KA10 6EF	11am - 4pm	40	Madabout ☎ 01294 835432
Sun 12th	Beijing Teddy Bear Show	798 Art District, Beijing	10am - 5pm	40	Taiwan Teddy Bear Association
Sun 19th	The Great Yorkshire Teddy Bear Event	Hilton Hotel, Victoria Quays, Sheffield, S4 7YB	10.30am - 3pm	58	Katie Rae Bears ☎ 07852 937518
Sun 26th	The Great Winter Doll & Teddy Fair	National Motorcycle Museum, Bickenhill, Nr Birmingham, B92 0EJ	10.30am - 4pm	Up to 90	Doll & Teddy Fairs ☎ 07973 760881

December 2017

Fri...Sun 1st	Hello Teddy!	Shopping Center Tishinka, Moscow	11am - 8pm	250	Antares Expo

February 2018

Sun 25th   Hugglets Winter   Kensington Town Hall,   10.30am - 4pm   175   WMM Publishing
                    BearFest 2018   Hornton St, London, W8 7NX   ☎ 01273 697974

March 2018

Sun 25th   The Great Spring   National Motorcycle Museum,   10.30am - 4pm   Up to   Doll & Teddy Fairs
                    Doll & Teddy Fair   Bickenhill, Nr Birmingham, B92 0EJ   90   ☎ 07973 760881

April 2018

Sat 4th   Pudsey Doll &   Pudsey Civic Hall, Pudsey,   10.30am - 4pm   Up to   Doll & Teddy Fairs
              Teddy Fair   Leeds, LS28 5TA   84   ☎ 07973 760881

Sun 8th   Newark   Cedric Ford Pavilion,   10.30am - 4pm   90+   Dolly's Daydreams
              Showground Event   Newark Showground, NG24 2NY   ☎ 01945 870160

Sat 14th   Artist Doll & Teddy   Clarion Hotel & Convention Center,   9am - 3pm   130   Susan Quinlan Doll &
              Bear Convention   Philadelphia International Airport   Teddy Bear Museum
                                                                            ☎ +1-805-687-8901

Sat 21st   Locks Heath   Lockswood Community Ctre,   11am - 4pm   40   Hants Events
              Teddy Bear Fair   Locks Heath, SO31 6DX   ☎ 07841 660177

Sat...Sun   TEDDYBÄR TOTAL   Halle Münsterland, Münster   Sat 10am - 5pm   280   Wellhausen & Marquardt
28/29th   Sun 11am - 4pm   Medien
                                                                          ☎ +49 40 42 91 77100

Sat...Sun   Spring DOLL Festival   Halle Münsterland, Münster   Sat 10am - 5pm   150   Wellhausen & Marquardt
28/29th   Sun 11am - 4pm   Medien
                                                                          ☎ +49 40 42 91 77100

May 2018

Sun 20th	Spring Hampshire Teddy Bear Festival	Lyndhurst Community Centre, SO43 7NY	10:30am - 4pm	45	Brewins' Bruins ☎ 01929 761398

July 2018

Sat...Sun 7th	Teddy Bear & Friends Convention	Bellesalle Takadanobaba, 3-8-2 Okubo, Shinjuku, Tokyo, 169-0072	11am - 5pm	250	Japan Teddy Bear Association
Sun 8th	The Great Stratford Teddy Bear Event	Stratford Arts House, 14 Rother Street, Stratford-upon-Avon, CV37 6LU	10.30am - 3pm	58	Katie Rae Bears ☎ 07852 937518

September 2018

Sun 9th	Hugglets Teddies Festival 2018	Kensington Town Hall, Hornton St, London, W8 7NX	10.30am - 4pm	175	WMM Publishing ☎ 01273 697974

FESTIVALS Hugglets TEDDIES FESTIVAL 2018

Sunday 9th September 2018 – exhibitor list at hugglets.co.uk
Kensington Town Hall, Hornton Street, London, W8 7NX

Sun 23rd	The Great Autumn Doll & Teddy Fair	National Motorcycle Museum, Bickenhill, Nr Birmingham, B92 0EJ	10.30am - 4pm	Up to 90	Doll & Teddy Fairs ☎ 07973 760881

October 2018

Sat 6th	Pudsey Doll & Teddy Fair	Pudsey Civic Hall, Pudsey, Leeds, LS28 5TA	10.30am - 4pm	Up to 84	Doll & Teddy Fairs ☎ 07973 760881
Sun 14th	Autumn Hampshire Teddy Bear Festival	Lyndhurst Community Centre, SO43 7NY	10:30am - 4pm	45	Brewins' Bruins ☎ 01929 761398
Sun 28th	Newark Showground Event	Cedric Ford Pavilion, Newark Showground, NG24 2NY	10.30am - 4pm	90+	Dolly's Daydreams ☎ 01945 870160

END

WINTER BEARFEST

Sunday, 25th February 2018

HUGGLETS
3 floors packed with bears

Twice a year Hugglets Festivals offer you over 170 stands in four bear-packed halls on three floors. Choose from 10.000 bears and related collectables on sale at each event. With four halls there's always something magical around the corner.

Kensington Town Hall
Hornton Street, London

Entry: 10:30am - 4:00pm
Tickets at door: £ 4 adult,
£ 2 child

Parking costs £10 for
9:00am - 6:00pm (400 spaces)

Nearest Tube is High Street Kensington
Venue postcode for satnav is W8 7NX

© Prue Theobalds

FESTIVALS Hugglets

WMM Publishing Ltd
St James House, 13 Kensington Square
London W8 5HD, United Kingdom

Phone: +44(0)20-77 95 81 33
Email: contact@hugglets.co.uk
Internet: www.hugglets.co.uk

The products on offer by any individual or company are listed in the belief that they are suitable for bearmaking.

However, no responsibility can be accepted by the publisher and readers must satisfy themselves on all matters regarding safety.

● BÄRENSTÜBCHEN BLÜMMEL
Jutta Blümmel, Kloppenheimer Str. 10, D-68239 Mannheim-Seckenheim, Germany
☎ +49 (0)621 4838812 mob: +49 (0)171 8253477
email: reginald.bluemmel@t-online.de
web: www.baerenstuebchen.de
Teddy bear materials and Steiff-Schulte fabrics.

● BEAR BASICS
☎ 01963 34500
email: enquiries@bearbasics.co.uk
web: www.bearbasics.co.uk
We supply bear makers in the UK and around the world. For all your bear making needs. See our display advert.

● BEAR WORKSHOPS BY THE SEA
Dymchurch, Kent
☎ 01303 870087
email: barbaraannbears@msn.com
web: www.barbara-annbears.com
Make a bear in sunny Kent. One-to-one tuition (or bring a friend). Tailor made for you. B&B available.

● BSB BEAR SUPPLIES
Sharon Aish, 107 Plymstock Road, Oreston, Devon, PL9 7PQ
☎ 01752 403515
email: bearlysanebears@sky,com
web: www.stores.ebay.co.uk/bsb-bear-supplies
We stock hand dyed mohair, bear making supplies and a range of my own patterns/kits. Visit our ebay shop.

● CHRISTIE BEARS LIMITED
Ref GD02, Office 5, Pyle Enterprise Centre, Village Farm Industrial Estate, Village Farm Road, Pyle, CF33 6BL
☎ 01656 670372
email: enquiries@christiebears.com
web: www.christiebears.com
Suppliers of fabrics, components and tools to teddy bear makers around the world.

● FANTASIA TEXTILES
Norah Stocker, Coggeshall Studio, Essex
☎ 01787 222946
email: norahjanet@hotmail.com
web: www.fantasiatextiles.co.uk
Textile artist, City & Guilds teacher, designer of teddies, quirky cloth dolls and lots more. Beautiful Monica Spicer patterns etc.

● G & T EVANS WOODWOOL
Dulas Mill, Mochdre Lane, Newtown, Powys, SY16 4JD
☎ 01686 622100 Fax: 01686 622220
email: gtevans1@aol.com
web: www.gtevans.co.uk
Manufacturers of superfine grades of wood wool for stuffing. Samples available. Call today for full details.

● PIPALUCK BEARS

16 Beechfield Road, Welwyn Garden City,
Hertfordshire, AL7 3RF
☎ 07966 162650
email: april@pipaluck.co.uk
web: www.pipaluck.co.uk
Miniature Bear Supplies. Full range of Sassy Fabrics in diverse spectrum of colours. Unique Artist Bears. Trusted seller since 2007.

● POLI PLASTIC PELLETS LTD

☎ 01244 940973
email: info@poliplasticpellets.com
web: www.poliplasticpellets.com
Stockists of a large selection of quality plastic pellets. Ideal for filling and weighting of dolls, bears, and other toys.

● TABBYCLOUDS

Leigh-on-Sea, Essex
☎ 07858 926591
email: tabbyclouds@btinternet.com
web: www.etsy.com/shop/TabbyClouds
Unique hand dyed Helmbold mohair and viscose. Many wonderful colours - pastels, brights, seasonal and more. Patterns and Kits also available.

● TEDDYTECH

PO Box 22377, Glenashley 4022, Kwa Zulu Natal, South Africa
☎ +27 (0)31 312 7755
email: info@teddytech.co.za
web: www.teddytech.biz
Where the magic of bearmaking begins. SA distributor of Schulte mohair, kits, patterns, bearmaking supplies.

● THE THROW COMPANY

The Design Studio, 12 Valleybridge Road,
Clacton-on-Sea, Essex, CO15 4AD
☎ 01255 475498
email: info@fauxthrow.com
web: www.fauxthrow.com
Fabulous faux furs, suedes etc., perfect for bear artists. Awards won with our fabrics. Wide selection, approx 73 faux furs. Swatches available.

END

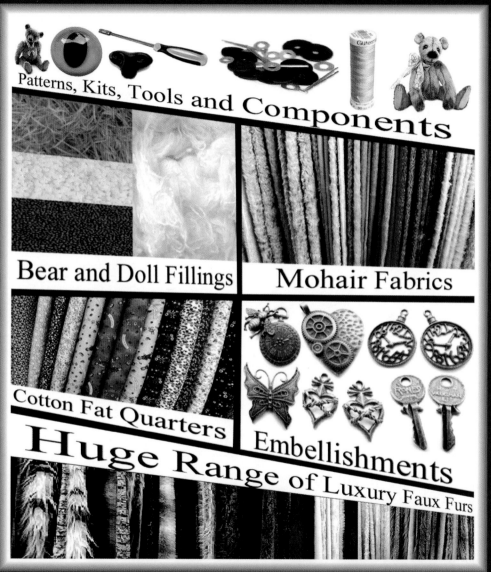

The following list of repairers is given in the belief that they are capable and experienced in their work. However, no responsibility is accepted for work carried out and readers must satisfy themselves on all such matters.

● AUSTROBEAR INTERNATIONAL

email: dolls@austrobear.co.uk
web: www.austrobear.co.uk

International Teddy and Doll repairer based in Cumbria. Website has information on Austrian teddies and examples of repairs.

● BA'S BEARS

5 Grove Street, Oxford, Oxfordshire, OX2 7JT
☎ 01865 435314
email: babruyn@hotmail.com
web: www.basbears.com

Sympathetic repair and restoration of mohair bears and friends. See web site for approximate costings.

● BEAR IT IN MIND

Hampshire
☎ mob: 07867 787795
email: info@bearitinmind.com
web: www.bearitinmind.com

On site restoration, cleaning and repair. Pop up clinics throughout the year. See our website for further details and venues.

● DOT BIRD

7 Tower Road, Ripon, North Yorkshire, HG4 1HP
☎ 01765 607131
email: dotsbears@btinternet.com

Specialising in sympathetic restoration of antique and vintage teddy bears. Meet me at the Hugglets fairs.

● BYGONE BEARS

17 Wyndham Road, Lower Parkstone, Poole, Dorset, BH14 8SH
☎ 01202 739926
email: bygonebears@gmail.com
web: www.bygone-bears.com

Careful and sympathetic restoration of vintage and antique teddy bears. See my website for photos, prices and FAQs.

● DUBEARS

57 Stretton Road, Morton, Alfreton, Derbyshire,
DE55 6GW
☎ 01773 590668 mob: 0789 1213335
email: gailmstorey@hotmail.co.uk

Any age bear carefully and lovingly repaired.

● EDENBEARS

Morecambe, Lancashire
email: edenvb@icloud.com
web: www.edenbears.co.uk

Sympathetic restoration of vintage mohair companions.
Work carried out with the greatest respect and care.
Detailed website including price guide.

END

This year we've reorganised the All Else section by moving museums to the old bears section and competitions to the Makers section.

● TEDDY BEAR PAINTINGS

Amanda Jackson, Elmhurst Lodge, Melton Mowbray, United Kingdom
☎ 01664 851314 mob: 07763 390299
email: aj@amandajackson.co.uk
web: www.amandajackson.co.uk
Outstanding original art, prints and cards by award winning painter Amanda Jackson.

Sophy G. Labbett

Pawtraits, Sketches, Cards, Mugs, Jigsaws, keyrings, jewellery, charms,and other bear stuff...

For more details contact me via Facebook or
slabbett23@gmail.com
Or via phone on **07860774464**

● BEARS&BUDS ONLINE MONTHLY TEDDY BEAR MAGAZINE

3428 Hillvale Road, Louisville, KY, 40241, USA
☎ +1 502 423 7827 mob: +1 502 548 2403 Fax: As tel.
email: bearsandbuds@aol.com
web: www.bearsandbuds.com
The original online teddy bear magazine featuring artists worldwide. Published monthly for 12 years. URSA Awards Competition Sponsor.

● CHRISTOPHER'S CHAIRS

Moreton, 30 Broadshard Lane, Ringwood, Hampshire, BH24 1RS
☎ 01425 475662
email: cdwhite@hotmail.co.uk
web: www.christopherschairs.co.uk
A wide range of handmade antique style Windsor chairs, rockers, highchairs and benches, for bears from 3 to 26.

● FANTASIA TEXTILES

Norah Stocker, Funky Dolls & Critters Club, at Coggeshall Studio, Essex
email: norahjanet@hotmail.com
web: www.fantasiatextiles.co.uk
Club meets periodically to learn how to design and create within the dolls world! Norah Stocker (Textile Artist).

● HANSA CREATION INC.

Action Agents Limited, 1 Georgian Close, Stanmore, Middlesex, HA7 3QT
☎ 020 8954 5956
email: info@hansa-uk.com
web: www.hansa-uk.com
WORLD-RENOWNED COLLECTION OF AMAZINGLY LIFE-LIKE (AND LIFE-SIZE), HAND-CRAFTED PLUSH ANIMALS.

● LA MODE POUR LES OURS

109 Knowles Hill, Rolleston on Dove, Burton on Trent, Staffs, DE13 9DZ
☎ mob: 07712 660582
email: enquiries@lamodepourlesours.co.uk
web: www.lamodepourlesours.co.uk
We make hand knitted, sewn and crocheted clothes and accessories for both 12 inch and 15 inch discerning teddy bears.

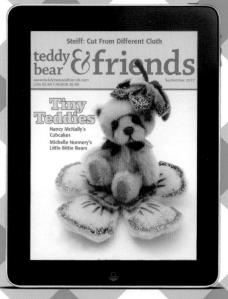

● PAT RUSH

36 The Chase, Racecourse Crescent, Shrewsbury, Shropshire, SY2 5BX
☎ 01743 231457
email: patrush9@icloud.com

Writer of four books and many hundreds of articles about Teddy Bears and other soft toys. British Bears a speciality.

● SOPHY LABBETT

29 Cloverfields, Horley, Surrey, RH6 0YJ
☎ 01293 862760 mob: 07860 774464
email: slabbett23@gmail.com
web: www.facebook.com/Sophy-G-Labbett-25499916787

Sketches, drawings, & watercolour pawtraits of bears & their friends.

● THE WAY OF THE BEAR

☎ mob: 07889 727087
email: norman@storybook.demon.co.uk
web: www.wayofthebear.net

A delightful book of photos and quotes by Author/Photographer Norman Silver to warm the hearts of young and old.

● WELLHAUSEN & MARQUARDT MEDIEN

Hans-Henny-Jahnn-Weg 51, Hamburg, 22085, Germany
☎ +49 (0)404291 77100 Fax: +49 (0)404291 77199
email: info@teddybaer-total.com
web: www.teddybaer-total.com

Publisher of TEDDYS kreativ and organiser of the TEDDYBÄR TOTAL show and the GOLDEN GEORGE awards.

END

ABC ~ Tedi Bach Hug

Bear Gallery

Welcome to our Gallery showcasing the wide variety of teddy bear styles available.

Please see the Bear Makers and Artists section for contact details (starting page 62).

Ann Made Bears

Arctophilia

Atelier Sigma

Baby Talk Bears by Soyo

Barron Bears

Bear Bits

Bearleigh Bears

Bearmore Bears

Bears by Karen

Bears by Sue Quinn

Bears 'N' Company

BeauT Bears by Marianne

Bell Bears

Bello-Born Bears

Benson Bears

Bisson Bears

Black Mountain Bears

Blinko Bears

BowerBird Bears

Bow Gussies

Bradgate Bears

Britannia Bears

FESTIVALS
Hugglets

Brotherwood Bears

Bumble Bears

Burlington Bearties

Carro Bears

Cama-Bären

Charlie Bears Ltd

Clemens Spieltiere

Dari Laut Bears

Dreli-Bären

D S-Bären

Edenbears

Everyn Rose

Frou-Frou

Futch Bears

Gill Dobson Bears

Grange Hollow Primitives

Haven Bears

Hidden Cove Bears

Hoblins

Huvi Bears

Jekabaer

Jenni Bears

Jodie's Bears

Ju-Beary Bears

Kaleideascope

KatieCountryBears

Kaz Bears

Koto Bears

Lake District Bears

Lefty Bears by Natascha Sabo

Little Piggies Originals

Live Toys by Olga Titova

Lolly Bou Creations

Lombard Bears

Lou's Loveables

Lovable Bears

Maisi-Baeren

Margarete Steiff UK

Marti creates

Merrythought

Miraberen

Moby and Puddle

Monton Bears

Muki Bear

My Apple Tree

Nana's Bear

Nessa Bears

Never Just A Bear

Nowhere Bears

Nyxy Nook

The Old Post Office Bears

O Little Shine Designs

Les Ours Tricotés

Padfield Bears

Pertinax Bears

Pipedream Bears

The Rabbit Maker

Samantha-jane Bears

Samt and Roses Bären

Sandra's Bärenbande

Shantock Bears

Shebob Bears

Julie Shepherd

Elena Stanilevici

StrawBeary Designs

Streete Bears

Sue's Ted's

Hugglets

Ted and Sue

Teddies Garden

Teddy Hermann

Teddy Ecke

Tellybears

ThimbleBeary Originals

ThreadTeds

Tickety Boo Bears

Toys, Stuffed and Handmade by Susan

Tweedies

Whittle-Le-Woods Bears

The Wild Things

END

Also including gollies, animals and other creations. International entries are indicated by a globe.

● A BEAR NAMED JACK

Christina Metcalfe
☎ mob: 07788 874888
email: abearnamedjack@gmail.com
web: www.abearnamedjack.co.uk
Come discover design, texture, and colour in every award winning creation. Follow us at facebook.com/ABearNamedJack to find Personality in Stitches!

● ABBY'S BEARS

Abby Aupiais, c/o 23 Carbis Road, Pietermaritzburg, South Africa
☎ +27 (0)72387 0576
email: ajaupiais@gmail.com
web: www.facebook.com/abbysbears
Handmade teddy bears, sew-alongs, bear-making fabrics and accessories.

● ABC ~ TEDI BACH HUG / DREAMTIME

Sue Woodhouse, 16 Innes Avenue, Telford, Shropshire, TF2 6BL
☎ 01952 270023
email: dreamtimer@gmail.com
web: http://abctbh.wix.com/abctbh
Award Winning Artist Miniatures ~ Wonderful bears and friends beautifully handmade. Hugglets Stand 138. Check website, blog/email for more details.

● ALL BEAR BY PAULA CARTER

21 Hazelwood Drive, Allington, Maidstone, Kent, ME16 0EA
☎ 01622 686970 mob: 07753 260001
email: allbearbypaula@gmail.com
web: www.allbearbypaula.com
Putting the Teddy back into Bear! Designer bears for the adult collector. Please visit the All Bear website!

● ALL THINGS BEARY

33 Pentland View, Edinburgh, Lothian, Scotland, EH10 6PY
☎ 0131 477 6970
email: hugs@allbeary.com
web: www.allbeary.com
Bears for all, many miniatures, themed bears, china, T-shirts, cards. Doll's house miniatures. Original designs. Website updated frequently. Mail order.

● AMY GOODRICH COLLECTABLES

Amy Goodrich's artistic creations
email: amygoodrich@gmx.com
web: www.amygoodrich.etsy.com
'Aristocratic amongst bears; The blue blood in your collection'©. View new creations. Email for news on showdates and stockists information.

● ANN MADE BEARS

Woollands, Tawton Lane, South Zeal, EX20 2LG
☎ 01837 849063
email: annreedsbears@gmail.com
Original handcrafted artist bears designed and made by Ann Reed. Available at bear fairs and by mail order. Commissions taken.

● ARCTOPHILIA

Unit 3, Horton Court, Hortonwood 50, Telford,
Shropshire, TF1 7GY
☎ 01952 604096
web: www.mohairbears.co.uk

Award winning heirloom collectable bears & dolls. Studio
based artist, designer & bear making tutor now hosting
regular group bear making courses.

● OLGA ARKHIPOVA

Moscow, Russia
☎ mob: +79151359778
email: proteddy@inbox.ru
web: www.proteddy.com

Let to introduce you intelligent, kind, dressed and shoed
artist handmade teddy bears. They are special with
exceptional own style.

● ART DOLL EXPO

(Shanghai Uideal Creative Design Service Co., Ltd.),
Amelia Wang, Room 434, Central Plaza, Huaqiao
International Service Business Park, Kunshan,
Jiangsu Province, 215332, China
☎ mob: +86 136 019 20831
email: artdollexpo@hotmail.com
web: www.artdoll-expo.com / VK: ART DOLL EXPO /
WeChat: artdollexpo

Organizer of ART DOLL EXPO in China, focusing on
market development and cultural communication of doll,
bear & small sculpture art.

● THE ARTFUL BEAR

Vivienne McBride, 7 Craigdimas Grove, Dalgety Bay,
Fife, KY11 9XR
☎ 01383 824306 mob: 07710 512998
email: info@theartfulbear.co.uk
web: www.theartfulbear.co.uk

Unique one-of-a-kind bears and other animals; handmade from Steiff Schulte mohair and luxury viscose.

● ATELIER SIGMA

Mika Fujita, Saitama, Japan
email: f-mika@mtb.biglobe.ne.jp
web: www.facebook.com/ateliersigma or www.
instagram.com/mika_sigma

Lifelike and beautiful bears from Japan. All handmade
by Mika Fujita. Please come and see them in the Winter
BearFest 2018.

⊙ ATELIER WIBA-BÄR

Ute Wilhelm & Lars Humme, Altstadt 1, 58636
Iserlohn, Germany
☎ +49 (0)2371 29845 mob: +49 (0)170 4111224
Fax: +49 (0)2371 14036
email: wiba-baer@web.de
web: www.atelier-wiba.de

Handmade and designed artist bears, clothes, decorations and accessories and much more. Please visit our website.

● AURORABEAREALIS

The Studio, Main Street, North Kessock, Inverness, Highland, IV1 3XN
☎ 01463 731110
email: susan@aurorabearealis.co.uk
web: www.aurorabearealis.co.uk

Miniature cotton patchwork bears and hares each one unique. Bear paintings, greetings cards and commissioned portraits as well.

● B'S BEARS

Karen Read, West Sussex
☎ mob: 07788 755882
email: karen@bsbears.co.uk
web: www.bsbears.co.uk

Beautiful handmade bears to love, hug and collect using the finest materials. Special orders welcome. Please check out my website.

⊙ BABY TALK BEARS BY SOYO

by Soyo Sato, Tokyo, Japan
☎ mob: +81 80 4422 7692
email: babytalk.bears@gmail.com
web: http://babytalkbears.moo.jp

OOAK artistic teddies.

● BARBARA-ANN BEARS

☎ 01303 870087
email: barbaraannbears@msn.com
web: www.barbara-annbears.com

One of a kind funky and traditional bears and kits, bear making classes, cards and website design.

● BARLING BEARS

by Marilyn Lambert, 13 Bear Tree Avenue, Ditton, Aylesford, Kent, ME20 6EB
☎ 01732 845059
email: marilyn@barlingbears.co.uk
web: www.barlingbears.co.uk

Wonderful hugs guaranteed with award winning Barling Bears. Individually designed and lovingly created using quality mohair/alpaca. Please see website.

● BARREL BEARS

69 Long Innage, Halesowen, West Midlands, B63 2UY
☎ mob: 07974 994302
email: mail@barrelbears.co.uk
web: www.barrelbears.co.uk

Award winning unique bears with needlefelted faces
and swivel ears. Mohair/faux fur/alpaca. Commissions
welcome. All bears cuddle tested. Restorations.

● BARRON BEARS

by Sharon Barron, 2296 Eastbrook Road, Vista, CA
92081, USA
☎ +1 760 598 9123
email: barrontb@gmail.com
web: www.barronteddiebears.com

Handmade and designed by artist Sharon Barron. Old
looking traditional bears, bear purses, big bears, and
much more.

● BEAN BRUINS

Linda Bean, Australia
email: linda@beanbruins.com
web: www.beanbruins.com

Handmade teddy bears, mohair bears, unique teddy
bears hand-made with love.

BARRON BEARS
by Sharon Barron

www.barronteddiebears.com

Bearleigh Bears
by Susan Leigh

Specializing in turning recycled fur coats into beautiful teddys

www.bearleighbears.com
susan@bearleighbears.com

From Fantasy to the Traditional Bear...

Https://m.facebook.com/bearmorebears/

By Sonia Beynon..

Sonz1974@hotmail.co.uk...... 0784 900 1528

● BEAR BITS

Ardgowan, Braehead, Avoch, Inverness, Highlands, IV9 8QL
☎ please see website
email: ashburner@bearbits.com
web: www.bearbits.com
Wonderful bears. See display advertisement.

● THE BEAR NECESSITIES – KNARF-BEARS

Groeninge 23, 8000 Brugge, Belgium
☎ +32 (0)5034 1027 Fax: As tel.
web: www.thebearnecessities.be
Artist bears by Maria Devlieghere. Beautiful original artist collector's bears from around the world. Unique Knarf Bears - limited editions.

● BEAR RHYMES

Marina Henman, 33, Calverley Road, Birmingham, B38 8PW
☎ mob: 07513645009
email: henman.marina@gmail.com
Bears of character, vintage looking bears, always one-of-a-kind and traditionally handmade

● BEARABLE BEARS

Anjo Noija, Burg. Jhr. Quarles van Uffordlaan 31, 7321 Z.S Apeldoorn, The Netherlands
☎ +31 (0)55 5788067
email: bearablebears@hotmail.com
web: www.facebook.com/anjomadebears
I hope my uniquely designed teddy bears can take you on a journey into the past.

● BEARLEIGH BEARS

1880 Pomeroy Road, Bannister, NSW 2580, Australia
☎ +61 (0)4 3801 6714
email: susan@bearleighbears.com
web: www.bearleighbears.com
Delightful collectable teddy bears made using only the finest quality fabric, including vintage, heirloom fur coats by Susan Leigh.

● BEARLYTHEREHUGS

Kathleen Eltis, 24 Shawbrow View, Bishop
Auckland, Co Durham, DL14 0XU
☎ 01388 602550 mob: 07467 950999
email: kathleen.eltis@sky.com
web: www.bearlytherehugs.jigsy.com
Wacky and colourful one-of-a-kind mohair fully jointed artist bears for the collector. Mail order.

● BEARMORE BEARS

Sonia Beynon
☎ mob: 07849 001528
email: sonz1974@hotmail.co.uk
web: www.facebook.com/bearmorebears /
http://twitter.com/sonia_beynon

Where new Beary Friends come to life in Luxury Faux
Furs and Mohairs. Traditional and Fantasy Commission
Orders Welcome, Hugs x

● BEARS 'N' COMPANY

Toronto, Canada
☎ +1 647 351 6427
email: ischmid@hotmail.com

Unique vintage looking bears. Please see display
advertisement.

● BEARS BY KAREN

Karen Graham, 1 Keltyhill Crescent, Kelty, Fife,
KY4 0LD
☎ mob: 07783 474259
email: karen_grahamuk@yahoo.co.uk
web: www.facebook.com/BearsByKaren

All my Bears are completely hand sewn by myself using
the finest materials. I also do commissions on request.

Bears 'N' Company
Ingrid Norgaard Schmid
email: ischmid@hotmail.com
telephone: 1617 828-2054

Bears by Karen
- Handmade in Scotland -

tel: 01383 839423
facebook.com/BearsByKaren

● BEARS BY SUE QUINN

Hunter House, 7 Hunter Street, Paisley,
Renfrewshire, Scotland, PA1 1DN
☎ 0141 887 9916
email: sue@bearsbysuequinn.co.uk
web: www.bearsbysuequinn.co.uk

Bears by Sue Quinn. Limited edition traditional jointed bears, dressed or undressed, in pure mohair and other quality fabrics.

● BEARS BY SUSAN JANE KNOCK

6 Elizabeth Avenue, Witham, Essex, CM8 1JE
☎ 01376 521230
email: susan.knock@tiscali.co.uk

Unique little character bears 1-7, also exquisite miniature range of 1 animals and toys. Please ring, email, sae for details.

● BEARS OF BATH

email: carol@bearsofbath.co.uk
web: www.bearsofbath.co.uk

Award winning artist bears, Tigers, Dragons, Mouse-bears & sculptured creations all hand sewn.

● BEARS UPON SOAR

Lisa Wills – Leicestershire UK
☎ 07866 616799
email: lisa@bearsuponsoar.co.uk
web: www.bearsuponsoar.co.uk

Creations inspired by real bears. Polars, Grizzlies and Black bears handcrafted using the highest quality materials by artist Lisa Wills.

● BEARS2HARES

Marilyn Grant, 138 Takeley Park, Hatfield
Broadoaks Road, Takeley, Essex, CM22 6TG
☎ mob: 07513 538807
email: bears2hares@yahoo.co.uk
web: www.facebook.com/Bears2hares

One of a kind handmade mohair bears and other critters. Small bears with big personalities. Photos on Facebook page.

● BEATRIX BEARS

283 Monkmoor Road, Shrewsbury, Shropshire,
☎ 01743 340276 mob: 07812 654405
email: beatrixharries60@gmail.com

Traditional and character artist bears. Worldwide delivery. All major credit cards accepted. Trade enquiries welcomed.

BEAUT BEARS

Bredenoord 206, 3079 JH Rotterdam, The
Netherlands
☎ +31 (0)610 623 559
email: beautbears@live.nl
web: www.beautbears.nl

Artist-designed handmade one-offs and custom-
made bears. Available on BearPile and fairs. See
advertisement and gallery.

● BEBBIN BEARS

by Yvonne Andrew, 7 Middle Road, Aylesbury,
Buckinghamshire, HP21 7AD
☎ 01296 423755
email: bebbinbears@gmail.com
web: www.bebbinbears.co.uk

Exquisite, unique, award winning artist bears,
designed and created for collectors. Each having
their own special character, personality, and
charm!

● BELL BEARS

The Workshop, 55 Tannsfeld Road, Sydenham,
London, SE26 5DL
☎ 020 8778 0217
email: bellbears@btinternet.com

Traditional collectors bears. For details and photographs,
please send £3 in stamps or cheque payable to Doreen
Bell. Commissions welcome.

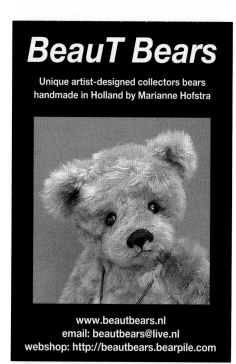

● BERTIE SWEEDLEPIPE BEARS

34 Peterborough road, Collingham, Newark,
NG23 7SP, Notts
☎ mob: 07854 359555
email: chez-paula@hotmail.co.uk
web: www.BertieSweedlepipeBears.bearpile.com

OOAK Bears and soft sculpture animals created
from the finest mohair or quality faux fur. Some are
extensively needlefelted to really give character to their
faces and paws.

● BISSON BEARS

Norway
☎ 0047 47834123
email: gailthornton@hotmail.com
web: www.facebook.com/BissonBears and
www.bissonbears.co.uk

**Traditionally designed and handmade limited
editions and one-of-a-kind collectors bears and
creatures by Gail Thornton.**

● BLACK MOUNTAIN BEARS

email: laurianne@blackmountainbears.co.uk
web: www.blackmountainbears.co.uk

Beautiful original hand knitted heirloom artist bears,
lovingly created from pure hand dyed fibres for you to
treasure.

● BLEE BEARS

16 Ellison Drive, Banbury, Oxfordshire, OX17 1GH
☎ 01295 258535
email: maria@bleebears.co.uk
web: www.bleebears.co.uk

One of a kind handmade artist bears. Commission
bears available.

● BLINKO BEARS

by Amanda Blinko, Wiltshire
☎ mob: 07799 660962
email: amandablinko@hotmail.co.uk
web: www.blinkobears.co.uk

Traditionally styled bears with personality, carefully
crafted using the finest materials.

● BOBBY'S BEARS

4 Station Road, Blackrod, Bolton, Lancashire,
BL6 5BN
☎ 01204 468090
email: bobbys.bears@uwclub.net
web: www.facebook.com/bobbysbears
Hand crafted traditional teddy bears.

● BOW GUSSIES

Cay Weightman, Granary Barn House, Hatfield Lane,
Hatfield, WR52PY
☎ 01905 312304 mob: 07769144257
email: karlandcarey@talktalk.net
web: www.bowgussies.bearpile.com
Antique replica bears of distinction – with all the
character and loving, but more weight.

● BOWERBIRD BEARS

The Red Hart, Llanvapley, Abergavenny, NP7 8SN
☎ mob: 07979 595397
email: gill@bowerbirdbears.co.uk
web: www.bowerbirdbears.co.uk
One of a Kind Teddy Bears hand made in Wales. 2017
Alfonzo Award Winner. Commissions undertaken, including Memory Bears.

Bow Gussies

Antique replica bears – with all the loving and more weight

bowgussies.bearpile.com

GOLDEN GEORGE

Giant sales show and family gathering on 28th-29th April 2018 in Münster, Germany

www.teddybaer-total.com

GOLDEN GEORGE

Feel the joy!

● BRADGATE BEARS

'The Lily Pot', 20 Ruskin Field, Anstey, Leicester,
LE7 7QP
☎ 0116 236 7147
email: judy@bradgatebears.co.uk
web: www.bradgatebears.co.uk
Bears of sweet nostalgia.

● BRIDGWATER BEARS

100 Bridgwater Road, Ipswich, Suffolk, IP2 9QF
☎ 01473 412066
email: rfdurrant@hotmail.co.uk
**Lots of new bears and old favourites all in super
mohair including many one offs.**

● BRIERLEY BEARS

86 Barnsley Road, Brierley, Barnsley,
South Yorkshire, S72 9JY
☎ 01226 714674 mob: 07841 159666
email: kat@brierleybears.co.uk
web: www.brierleybears.co.uk
Award winning OOAK artist bears designed and
handmade by Kat Hartley. Made only from the finest
materials. Commissions welcome.

● BRITANNIA BEARS

by Karen Elderfield, Wisbech, Cambs
☎ 01945 475197
email: kelderfield@aol.com
web: www.britanniabears.co.uk /
www.facebook.com/britanniabears-339979626100645
/ www.instagram.com/britanniabears
Distinctive, traditional style bears with a touch of old charm
about them. Lovingly created with the finest of materials.

● BROTHERWOOD BEARS

15 Saxon Street, Chippenham, Wiltshire, SN14 0LP
☎ 01249 322300
email: suebrotherwood@sky.com
web: www.brotherwoodbears.com
Original one-off Fairy Bears, or visit my website to see
my bears acclaimed for their lovable faces and charm -
or visit my sweet shop for a treat!

● BUMBLE BEARS

17 Adur Close, West End, Southampton, Hampshire,
SO18 3NH
☎ 02380 326663
email: bumblebears95@gmail.com
web: www.bumble-bears.com
Traditional collectors bears by Fiona Wells, designed and
handmade with great care and attention to detail, since
1995. See advertisement.

**Bradgate Bears
by Judy Follows**

www.britanniabears.co.uk
kelderfield@aol.com
01945475197

britanniabears
By
Karen Elderfield

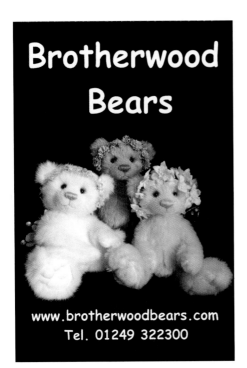

Brotherwood Bears

www.brotherwoodbears.com
Tel. 01249 322300

● BUMBLY BEARS
34 Maple Avenue, Baglan, Port Talbot, West Glamorgan, SA12 8LY
☎ 01639 813514
email: dianesouthall@ntlworld.com
web: www.bumblybears.co.uk / www.facebook.com/BumblyBears
Traditional and wacky collectors bears. All one offs in mohair and faux fur. See website for details and fair dates.

● BURLINGTON BEARTIES
2 Ambergate Drive, Kingswinford, West Midlands, DY6 7HZ
☎ 01384 279731
email: burlingtonbearties@googlemail.com
Antique style realistic characters for collectors. Bears, cats and rabbits all individually dressed in vintage clothing.

● CAMA - BAEREN
Carmen Matte, Hauptstraße 32, 97708 Großenbrach, Germany
email: c-matte@t-online.de
web: www.camabaeren.de
Hand sewn bears, all are made to look old. All bears are One - offs.

Bumble Bears
by Fiona Wells

Tel: 02380 326663
www.bumble-bears.com
email: bumblebears95@gmail.com
www.folksy.com/shops/BumbleBearsandDesigns

BURLINGTON BEARTIES

Telephone for details
**2 Ambergate Drive, Kingswinford,
W. Midlands, DY6 7HZ Tel: 01384 279731
Email: burlingtonbearties@googlemail.com**

CARROBEARS

Caroline Ackermann, Violgatan 4, 59932 Ödeshög,
Sweden
☎ +46 (0)70 320 22 62
email: ackermann@telia.com
web: www.facebook.com/CarroBears
Handcrafted OOAK-bears and other beary things. Please
see display advertisement and Bear Gallery picture.
Please visit CarroBears on Facebook.

● CATERHAM YESTERBEARS

☎ 01883 346107 (Carolyn) mob: 07837 842948 (Clare)
email: caterhamyesterbears@gmail.com
web: http://yesterbears.blogspot.co.uk
Hand stitched traditional mohair bears and buddies.
Many OOAK's. From 10 cm. Check blog for new designs.

● CHARLIE BEARS LIMITED

The Bearhouse, Pipers Close, Pennygillam Ind Est,
Launceston, Cornwall PL15 7PJ
☎ 01566 777092
email: sales@charliebears.com
web: www.charliebears.com
Affordable and highly collectable, Charlie Bears are
known as the bears with personalities. Designed by bear
artists, made by hand.

● CHATHAM VILLAGE BEARS L.L.C.

Artist Art Rogers, 3300 Duck Ave, Key West,
FL 33040, USA
☎ +1 314 566 2940
email: geoart1@swbell.net
web: www.chathamvillagebears.com
Art is constantly creating something new to keep his
collectors wondering what will come next. Please see the
website and go to the Pinterest page for new arrivals.

● CHELTENHAM BEARS

7 Edendale Road, Golden Valley Park, Cheltenham,
Gloucestershire, GL51 0TX
☎ mob: 07905 307859
email: suerowe@ip3.co.uk
web: www.cheltenhambears.co.uk
Beautiful mohair bears, hand stitched to highest quality
by Sue. Visit my online shop. Commissions taken.

● CLAUDINOURS

Claudine Lamontre, 12 rue de Chaumont, 52310 Marault, France
☎ +33 (0)325 324 706 mob: +33 (0)685 488 089
email: claudine.prignet@wanadoo.fr
web: www.claudinours.sitew.com
Bespoke hand-made traditional teddy bears.

● CLEMENS BEARS OF GERMANY

c/o A M International Agencies Ltd., Digital House, Peak Business Park, Foxwood Rd, Chesterfield, Derbyshire, S41 9RF
☎ 01246 269723 Fax: 01246 269724
email: enquiries@am-international-agencies.com
web: www.clemens-spieltiere.de
World famous traditional and artist bears from Germany's leading company, Clemens. Finest quality mohair and the most appealing bears guaranteed!

● CLUMSY BEARS

Marcia Hastings, 113 Arthurton Road, Spixworth, Norwich, Norfolk, NR10 3QX
☎ 07789 392235
email: info@clumsybears.co.uk
web: www.clumsybears.co.uk
Designed and handmade by Marcia using a range of fabrics and colours. Some are more Clumsy than others!

● CODENAME BUTTERFLY

Katya Gless
☎ mob: 07341 656302
email: codenamebutterflyshop@gmail.com
web: www.codenamebutterfly.com
Ooak bears and creatures. Each creation has a distinct character and look. Visit the website to see more.

● COLLECTOR BUTTON BEARS

Brenda MacKinnon, Meadow Edge House, Deighton, North Yorkshire, DL6 2SJ
email: buttonbears@btinternet.com
web: www.collectorbuttonbears.co.uk
Bears and creatures made with love for the collector.

● CONRADI CREATIONS

☎ mob: 07070000110
email: karin@conradicreations.com
web: www.conradicreations.com / www.facebook.com/ConradiCreations
Traditional mohair & alpaca collectors bears. Designed and handsewn by award-winner Karin Conradi. Special commissions welcomed & layaway available.

● COWSLIP BEAR COMPANY

2 Warren Avenue, Mudeford, Christchurch, Dorset, BH23 3JX
☎ 01202 382073 or 07776 108528
email: cowslipbears@ntlworld.com
web: www.cowslipbears.co.uk
Mohair bears 8 to 31 made to order for any occasion. Crystal bears 8 available. Please specify crystal.

● THE CREATIVE TEDD

12 Kime Mews, Kirton, Boston, Lincolnshire, PE20 1LP
☎ mob: 07859 001340
email: thecreativetedd@gmail.com
web: www.thecreativetedd.co.uk
Bespoke bears and dolls lovingly created from quality materials by Clare Davis-Tedd. Enquiries welcome.

● CROTCHETY BEARS

4 Spring Grove Crescent, Kidderminster, Worcestershire, DY11 7JB
☎ 01562 752289
email: crotchetybear@gmail.com
Collectors teddy bears and pandas. Original designs hand made by Chris in traditional materials.

● CUDDLEKIN BEARS

57 Derham Gardens, Upminster, RM14 3HB
☎ mob: 07930 247948
email: cuddlekinbears@gmail.com
web: www.cuddlekinbears.co.uk
Natural style bears in mohair and alpaca. Handmade and designed by Kiyomi.

● CUPBOARD BEARS

by Elizabeth Lloyd, 11 Rowan Close, Highcliffe, Dorset, BH23 4SW
☎ 01425 838342
email: cupboardbears@hotmail.com
web: http://cupboardbears.blogspot.co.uk
Artist bears of distinction since 1994. Join my mailing list for regular updates.

● D AND A BEARS

Diane Jones, 7 Borrowdale Grove, Northfield, Birmingham, B31 5QN, United Kingdom
☎ mob: 07803 092563
email: dandabears@gmail.com
web: www.dandabears.uk
Handmade teddy bears, original designs, OOAK in mohair or plush, traditionally jointed. Created with love by Diane Jones. Enquiries welcome.

BEARS WITH PERSONALITIES

Join the Charlie Bears Best Friends Club for sneaky peeks of new collections, secret cupboard exclusives & many more bear-illiant benefits...

Contact the bear cubs at The Bearhouse to become one of our Best Friends!

Charlie Bears Ltd
The Bearhouse | Pipers Close | Pennygillam Ind. Estate | Launceston | Cornwall PL15 7PJ
T 01566 777 092 **E** headbear@charliebears.com **www.charliebears.com**

Dari Laut Bears

by Award Winning Artist

Traditional and character bears and animals. Dressed and undressed.

Designed and lovingly created by Patricia Banks

Tel: 01424 754418

www.dari-laut-bears.co.uk

Email: pat@dari-laut-bears.co.uk

● DANDELION BEAR ORPHANS

☎ mob: 07526 500182
email: dandelionbears@mail.com
web: www.dandelionbears.bearpile.com

100% handstitched OOAK whimsical teddy bears and critters made by Traceyann Papworth on the Isle of Wight. Custom orders welcomed.

● DARI LAUT BEARS

Dari Laut, 25 De Chardin Drive, Hastings, East Sussex, TN34 2UD
☎ 01424 754418
email: pat@dari-laut-bears.co.uk
web: www.dari-laut-bears.co.uk

Traditional and character bears and animals designed and lovingly created by award winning artist Patricia Banks. Enquiries welcome. Photographs available.

● DEB CANHAM ARTIST DESIGNS

216 Highpoint Drive, Venice, FL, 34292, USA
email: deb@debcanham.com
web: www.debcanham.com

Specializing in limited edition collectible fabric figurine animals from 3cm – 45cm. Deb Canham Studio – original one of a kind pieces.

● DRELI-BEARS & DRAGONS

by Andrea Maria Mazzitelli-Köhler, Rifer-Hauptstrasse 76/Top 3, 5400 Hallein RIF, Austria
☎ +43 (0)664 412 4671
email: andrea@mazzitelli.at
web: www.mazzitelli.at

Handmade bears, mohair and longpile, Dragons richly decorated with pearls, entirely handmade of velvet, fully wired, waiting for lovely homes.

● DS-BÄREN

by Dagmar Seibel, Kardinal-Wendel-Str, 11, D-67487 Maikammer, Germany
☎ 00 49/63 21 597 35
email: ds-baeren@t-online.de
web: www.ds-baeren.de

Teddy bears with unique expressions - designed by Dagmar Seibel and crafted from high quality material

Dagmar Seibel
www.ds-baeren.de

Frou - Frou

www.frou-froubears.com
teenabasy@gmail.com

◉ ECOBEARS

C/San Sebastian 89, Urb. La Marina,
San Fulgencio, Alicante, 03177, Spain
☎ 00 44 (0) 7486860899
email: ecobears@hotmail.com /
Facebook/Twitter @Ecobears
web: www.ecobears.com
Ecobears and character friends from planet
Vynen. OOAKs hand made with love and attention
– all from the very best materials.

● EDENBEARS

Morecambe, Lancashire
email: edenvb@icloud.com
web: https://edenvb.wixsite.com/mysite
One of a kind designs, traditional, jointed, mohair
collector bears. Made with great care and attention to
detail. Commissions welcome.

◉ ELLE ET L'OURS

Sandrine Pichard, La Grouas, 72240 Ruillé en
Champagne, France
☎ +33 688 312591
email: elleetlours@nordnet.fr
web: www.elleetlours.jimdo.com

● ELLIEBEARS

272 Southend Rd, Wickford, Essex, SS11 8PS
☎ 01268 762438
email: ellie.covell@blueyonder.co.uk
Loveable collectors mohair and alpaca artist bears and
Furry Friends carefully created. Commissions welcome.

◉ EVERYN ROSE

2-2-25, Saihiro, Icihara-shi, Chiba 290-0022, Japan
☎ +81 (0)436 22 6823
email: everynrose@yahoo.co.jp
web: www.facebook.com/masako.kitao
I have been creating animals such as teddy bears, bunnies and cats since 2002. Award winning artist Masako
Kitao.

● FANTASIA TEXTILES

Norah Stocker, Coggeshall Studio, Essex
☎ 01787 222946
email: norahjanet@hotmail.com
web: www.fantasiatextiles.co.uk
Artist of miniature and medium size teddy bears. Also
wonderful quirky fabric dolls. Quilts and wall hangings.
City & Guilds teacher.

● FLOPSEY BEARS

by Carole Oliver
☎ mob: 07818 037662
email: carole@flopseybears.com
web: www.flopseybears.com

Unique handmade bears and friends. Featuring heavily weighted limbs making them gorgeously 'flopsey', enabling them to sit and hang in various poses.

● FLUTTER-BY BEARS

by Ruth Bowman, 26 Ludford Close,
Newcastle-under-Lyme, Staffordshire, ST5 7SD
☎ 01782 560136
email: ruthbowman@tiscali.co.uk
web: www.flutter-by-bears.co.uk

Award winning miniature artist bears and friends. Designed to delight, sewn with love to be exquisite. Have a tiny hug!

● FROU-FROU

Christeena-Marie Bas, Sandside, 37 Rugeley Road,
Hazelslade, Staffs, WS12 0PH
☎ 01543 426661
email: teenabasy@gmail.com
web: www.frou-froubears.com

Traditional Bears made with the finest mohair, in beautiful clothing with a Frou-Frou of antique materials, trims, frills and adornments.

● FUTCH BEARS

☎ mob: 07930 335192
email: difutcher@dsl.pipex.com
web: www.futchbears.co.uk

Artist bears with antique accessories.

● GARJAR BEARS

Jacqueline Roughead
email: garjarbears@gmail.com
web: garjarbears.wixsite.com/garjarbears

OOAK Artist Bears designed and lovingly handsewn by myself using the finest materials. Commissions welcome. More details on Facebook/website.

● GILL DOBSON TEDDY BEARS

29 Crabmill Lane , Easingwold, North Yorkshire,
YO613DF
☎ 01347823122
email: gilldobson@ymail.com
web: www.gilldobsonteddybears.co.uk

Gill's bears are crafted from the best materials and cleverly detailed to create characters that will be treasured for generations.

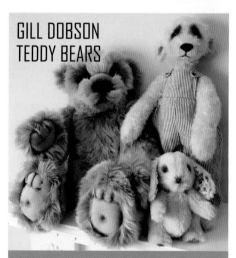

Traditional bears, folk art and primitive creations, handcrafted in Kent by **Ellen Wright**

www.grangehollow.com
email: ellen@grangehollow.com

HAVEN BEARS

Tel: 07948 200031
email: info@havenbears.co.uk
web: www.havenbears.co.uk

● GOLD TEDDY BEARS

60 Mortimer Avenue, Batley, West Yorkshire, WF17 8BU
☎ 01924 420272
email: joan@goldteddy.co.uk
web: www.goldteddy.co.uk and www.lynnetteweaver.co.uk

Gorgeous handmade mohair bears from Joan's original, exclusive designs. Beautiful bear portraits available by artist Lynnette Weaver. Commissions taken.

● GOLDEN GEORGE

Wellhausen & Marquardt Medien, Hans-Henny-Jahnn-Weg 51, Hamburg, 22085, Germany
☎ +49 (0)404291 77100 Fax: +49 (0)404291 77199
email: info@teddybaer-total.com
web: www.golden-george.com and www.teddybaer-total.com

The renowned GOLDEN GEORGE is one of the most important awards for international bear artists and will be awarded at TEDDYBÄR TOTAL.

● GRANGE HOLLOW

48 Grange Road, Gillingham, Kent, ME7 2PU
☎ 01634 570331 mob: 07890 002153
email: ellen@grangehollow.com
web: www.grangehollow.com

Traditional handcrafted bears, folk art and primitive creations by Kent artist Ellen Wright.

● JO GREENO

2 Woodhill Court, Woodhill, Send, Surrey, GU23 7JR
☎ 01483 224312
email: jo.greeno@btinternet.com

International artist and designer specialising in one of a kind dressed bears and animals. Established 1990.

● GYLL'S BEARS

74 Kenilworth Crescent, Enfield, Middlesex, EN1 3RG
☎ 020 8366 1836
email: gyllsbears@hotmail.co.uk
web: www.gyllsbears.bearpile.com

Handmade mohair bears.

● HAJA-BEARS

Bettekamp 79, Ede, Gelderland, 6712 EJ, The Netherlands
☎ +31 (0)318 619103
email: info@haja-bears.com
web: www.haja-bears.com

Handmade collectable bears & critters in minifabrics and threads. Also supplying thread, accessories and my own crochet pattern designs.

● HANDMADE KEEPSAKE RAG DOLLS AND COLLECTABLES

by Angela Holt, 38 Lyddesdale Ave, Thornton Cleveleys, Blackpool, Lancs, FY5 3EH
☎ mob: 07432 732691
email: angelaholt2002@yahoo.co.uk
web: www.facebook.com/HandmadeKeepsakeRagDollsandcollectables

Featured Bear artist in The Guild of Master Bearcrafters Also, a featured Bear Artist in TEDDYzine, an online German magazine.

● HANSA CREATION INC.

Action Agents Limited, 1 Georgian Close, Stanmore, Middlesex, HA7 3QT
☎ 020 8954 5956
email: info@hansa-uk.com
web: www.hansa-uk.com

WORLD-RENOWNED COLLECTION OF AMAZINGLY LIFE-LIKE (AND LIFE-SIZE), HAND-CRAFTED PLUSH ANIMALS.

● HARDY BEARS

by June Kendall, 106 Oakbury Drive, Preston, Weymouth, Dorset, DT3 6JH
☎ 01305 835435   mob: 0797 9032 994
email: junelkendall@btinternet.com

Established bear artist. Quality bears 10-20cm handmade by June Kendall. Special orders and repairs welcome.

● HAVEN BEARS

☎ 07948 200031
email: info@havenbears.co.uk
web: www.havenbears.co.uk

Handmade 'one of a kind' alpaca and mohair bears, from 3 1/2 to 21 tall. Made in the heart of Cheshire.

● HERMANN TEDDY ORIGINAL

Teddy-Hermann GmbH, Postfach 1207, D-96112 Hirschaid, Germany
☎ +49 (0)9543 84820   Fax: +49 (0)9543 848210
email: info@teddy-hermann.de
web: www.teddy-hermann.de

Traditional mohair bears in limited editions, miniatures and high-quality plush animals in naturalistic designs. UK Main Agent: Brian Somers. Tel: 020 8954 5956. Please see advertisement on page 87.

● HERMANN TEDDY ORIGINAL

UK Main Agents Brian and Myrna Somers, 1 Georgian Close, Stanmore, Middlesex, HA7 3QT
☎ 020 8954 5956
email: myrna@actionagentsltd.com
web: www.teddy-hermann.de
Please see advertisement on page 87.

● HIDDEN COVE BEARS

☎ 01626 853251
email: hiddencovebears@googlemail.com
web: www.hiddencovebears.co.uk

Hand sewn mohair bears created by Margaret Corbett and inspired by my love of bears in the wilds of Canada.

● HIGGYS BEARS

☎ 01323 841819
email: emelia@higgysbears.co.uk
web: www.higgysbears.co.uk

Higgys Bears, one of a kind Traditional and Vintage style artist bears lovingly created every time xx by Emelia Pollard.

● HOBLINS

5 Byron Avenue, Warton, Preston, Lancashire, PR4 1YR
☎ 01772 635516
email: hoblins.bears@btinternet.com

Lovely outfits or just bare, weighty mohair bears from four to twenty inches. All handmade in Lancashire by Linda Willetts.

HOLLINFARE BEARS

K Twigg, Warrington, Cheshire
☎ mob: 07708 983895
email: hollinfarebears@hotmail.com
web: www.hollinfarebears.webs.com
One of a kind traditional mohair hand stitched jointed bears.

HOLLY BEARS

Rosebank Cottage, 70 Heath Road, Uttoxeter, Staffordshire, ST14 7LT
☎ 01889 568848
email: hollybears@tiscali.co.uk
Handmade one-off bears.

HONEYDEW BEARS

27 Boerneef Street, Helderkruin, Gauteng, South Africa
☎ +27 (0)11 764 4317
email: info@honeydewbears.co.za
web: www.honeydewbears.co.za
Wonderful selection of teddy bear kits, mohair, eyes, joints, patterns etc. Best kits by far! We ship Internationally. Look out for our Etsy shop soon.

HOVVIGS

Yvonne Graubaek, Hovvigvej 68, 4500 Nykoebing Sj, Denmark
☎ +45 5991 3494
email: hovvigs@post.tele.dk
Please see display advertisement.

PAM HOWELLS

39 Frognall, Deeping St James, Peterborough, Cambridgeshire, PE6 8RR
☎ 01778 344152
Quality traditional teddy bears. Hand crafted from the finest mohair. Limited edition collectors' bears and award winning exclusive soft toys.

HUGGY BEARS UK

117 Diamond Avenue, Kirkby-in-Ashfield, Nottinghamshire, NG17 7LX
☎ 01623 458514 mob: 07796 952427
email: bonniray@yahoo.co.uk
web: www.facebook.com/HuggyBearsUK
5 to 15 vintage style bears including soldiers and nurses. Knitted and sewn outfits available. Jointed gollies with crazy hair.

HUGOSHOUSE

Gregory Gyllenship, 5 Primrose Road, Walton-on-Thames, Surrey, KT12 5JD
☎ 01932 243263
email: gregory@hugoshouse.com
web: www.hugoshouse.com
Bears designed and individually made by Gregory Gyllenship.

HUWI BEARS

Corinne Locher-Huwyler, Dorfstrasse 11, 4932 Gutenburg, Switzerland
☎ mob: 0041 79 453 19 61
email: huwibears@besonet.ch
web: www. Huwibears.ch
Huwibears designed and created with Love by Corinne Locher Huwyler

JAN'S TIDDY BEARS

2 Maritime Court, Blenheim Road, Epsom, Surrey, KT19 9AP
☎ mob: 07889 794637
email: janstiddybears@gmail.com
Award winning miniature bear artist. Lovingly designed and hand sewn miniatures by Jan. One to four inches. Commissions taken.

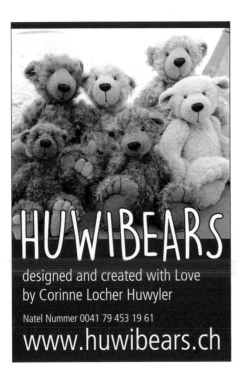

16655 9
Lauritz, 54 cm
with growler
LE 200 pcs.

15610 9
Lucky Charm
Teddy
Chimney Sweep, 15 cm
LE 300 pcs.

16820 1
Traditional
Teddy, 27 cm
LE 400 pcs.

15488 4
Antique Bear
light-gold, 10 cm

15489 1
Antique Bear
taupe, 10 cm

LE 200 pcs ea.

HERMANN *Teddy* ORIGINAL®

The Teddy-Hermann Collectors' Club unites bear friends worldwide since its start in the year 2000.
Join our Collectors' Club now and become also a member of the big Teddy-Hermann family.

An exclusive gift awaits you: a high-quality "HERMANN Teddy ORIGINAL" Bear
of 13 cm size. You have the right to acquire an Exclusive Club Edition which is
only available to members of the Teddy-Hermann Collectors' Club and receive
twice a year our newsletter called "Barenpost" as well as our latest catalogues
and updates. For further information please contact your Teddy-Hermann stockist
and ask for an application form to join the Club.

Teddy-Hermann GmbH
Postfach 1207 D-96112 Hirschaid Germany
www.teddy-hermann.de

Club Gift 2017
13 cm

UK Main Agent: Brian & Myrna Somers, 1 Georgian Close, Stanmore, Middx, HA7 3QT
Tel: 0208 954 5956 email: myrna@actionagentsltd.com

 http://www.facebook.com/TeddyHermannGmbH

JEKABAER

Jeannette Kasel
Varmisser Strasse 8, 37127 Dransfeld
Germany · Mob: 00 49/151/21 73 97 87
email: teddymacherin@web.de · web: www.jekabaer.de

Big and miniature artistical Teddys/Animals with high quality and own designs/cuts. No standart produktion, it´s boring. Unikate.

One of a kind hand sewn bears and critters by Jean · Traditional & modern ·

● JCW BEARS & FURRY FRIENDS

11 Cockerell Close, Pitsea, Basildon, Essex, SS13 1QR
☎ 01268 726558
email: jacquiwickenden@hotmail.co.uk
web: www.jcwbears.co.uk
Award winning character bears, realistic dogs, cats & other furry friends exclusively designed and made by Jacqui Wickenden.

● JEKABAER

Jeannette Kasel, Varmisser Strasse 8, 37127 Dransfeld, Germany
☎ mob: 00 49/151/21 73 97 87
email: teddymacherin@web.de
web: www.jekabaer.de
Big and miniature artistical Teddys/Animals with high quality and own designs/cuts. No standart produktion, it´s boring. Unikate.

● JENNI BEARS

5 Copperfield Road, Poynton, Stockport, Cheshire, SK12 1LX
☎ 01625 877184
email: jennibears@aol.com
web: www.jennibears.co.uk
Hand sewn unique artist bears in mohair or alpaca. Traditional or modern. All born in need of love and cuddles!

● JINNEE BEARS OF EXETER

Jane Natolie, 1A Commins Road, Exeter, EX1 2QB
☎ 01392 257315 mob: 07760 204394
email: sales@jinneebearsofexeter.co.uk
web: www.jinneebearsofexeter.co.uk
Hand sewn, traditional style, fully jointed, individual bears. Made from mohair and other furs and fabrics. Cute and cuddly.

● JODIE'S BEARS

Tomoko Suenaga, 3-28-1 Kataseyama, Fujisawa, Kanagawa, 251-0033, Japan
☎ +81 (0)466 25 1202 Fax: +81 (0)466 27 2260
email: jodie@teddiebear.jp
Enjoy the fairylike bears with me at Teddies 2018!

● JOXY BEARS

31 Gowerby Hoode, Bridlington, East Yorkshire, YO16 7DE
☎ 01262 679688
email: josymon@hotmail.co.uk
web: www.joxybears.com
Original bears, pandas, dogs and other critters lovingly hand sewn from tip to toe by Jo.

● JU-BEARY BEARS

5 Deirdre Avenue, Wickford, Essex, SS12 0AX
☎ mob: 07711 191241
email: jubearybears@hotmail.co.uk
web: www.jubearybears.com

Award winning OOAK artist bears and friends. Original
designs, made from the finest mohair and alpaca. See
photo in Bear Gallery.

● JUST BEARS UK

Yvonne Lehman, The Emporium, 39 Princes Street,
Yeovil, Somerset, BA20 1EG
☎ mob: 07736 320011
web: www.justbearsuk.co.uk

See us on Facebook. Steiff, Charlie Bears,Artist Bears
and more. Can also order online for delivery UK and
Overseas.

● K.M. BEARS

by Kerren Morris, 66 Kirklees Drive, Farsley,
Pudsey, West Yorkshire, LS28 5TE
☎ 0113 2299 899
email: kerren@kmbears.co.uk
web: www.kmbears.co.uk

Beautiful handmade bears. Commissions undertaken.

● KALEIDEASCOPE

Francesca Boretti, Habsburgerstrasse 38, 4310
Rheinfelden, Switzerland
☎ +41 (0)61 8310444 mob: +41 774726342
email: francesca.boretti@gmail.com
web: www.kaleideascope.net

OOAK realistic soft sculpture animals lovingly designed
and hand crafted by Italian artist Francesca Boretti.

● KAREN ALDERSON ARTIST DESIGN

P.O. Box 224, Gembrook, VIC 3783, Australia
email: karen@karensdolls.com
web: www.karenalderson.com/bears

Small and miniature Artist bears with a girly vintage
touch, Handmade from the finest materials.

● NATASHA KATAEVA

614002 Perm, Ostrovskogo 70-160, Russia
☎ +7 342 216 74 75 mob: +7 908 27 623 19
email: teddyclub@mail.ru

Vintage and classic teddy bears from the middle of
Russia.

Jodie's Bears
by Tomoko Suenaga

jodie@axel.ocn.ne.jp

KALEideaSCOPE
by Francesca Boretti

www.KALEideaSCOPE.net

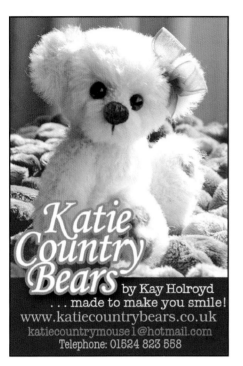

● **KATIECOUNTRYBEARS**
81 Greenwood Avenue, Bolton-Le-Sands, Carnforth, Lancashire, LA5 8AW
☎ 01524 823558
email: katiecountrymouse1@hotmail.com
web: www.katiecountrybears.co.uk
Handmade mohair, alpaca and plush bears, lovingly made to put a smile on your face. Created by Kay Holroyd.

● **KAYANNE KREATIONS**
by Ann Lown, 23 Alanbrooke Grove, Lightwood, ST3 7ES
☎ 01782 912957 mob: 07737 476977
email: ann@kayannekreations.co.uk
web: www.kayannekreations.co.uk
We are a mother and daughter business creating crochet and needle felted bears and other cute creations and gifts.

● **KAYCEE BEARS™**
Kelsey Cunningham, The Studio, The Old School House, Yarburgh, Louth, Lincolnshire, LN11 0PW
☎ 01507 363955 mob: 07415 122688
email: kayceebears@gmail.com
web: www.kayceebears.co.uk
The finest handmade teddy bears and dragons. All handmade in England.

● **KAYSBEARS BY KAY STREET**
93 Singlewell Road, Gravesend, Kent, DA11 7PU
☎ 01474 351757 Fax: 01322 521746
Award winning miniature bears, made with love.

● **KAYTKINS BEARS**
Kayt Iles
☎ 01933 355782 mob: 07887 877181
email: kaytkinsbears@hotmail.com
web: www.facebook.com/kaytkins.bears
Affordable bears and friends designed and handmade in Northamptonshire. Commissions welcome.

● **KAZ BEARS**
70 Lindon Drive, Alvaston, Derby, Derbyshire, DE24 0LN
☎ 01332 731948
email: kazbears@ntlworld.com
web: www.kazbears.com
Traditional and old looking bears with a soulful look, made from quality mohair, collectable and appealing to all.

● KEVINTON BEARS

12 Stanley Street, Caterham, Surrey, CR3 5JY
email: mail@kevintonbears.com
web: www.kevintonbears.com &
www.facebook.com/kevintonbears

**Cute and little Teddy Bear friends handmade by
artist Hazel Dancey. Please visit my website and
facebook page. Thank you!**

● KNOCKIE BEARS BY SLACKSTITCHES

Margaret Hamilton, Slack Villa, 23 King Edward
Terrace, Portknockie, Banffshire, AB56 4NX
☎ 01542 840551 mob: 07855 249667
email: margaret@slackstitches.com
web: www.slackstitches.com

Individually handmade bears in Scotland from Scottish
tartan, tweed and knitted fabrics.

● KÖSEN UK

Silver Ley, The Highlands, East Horsley, Surrey,
KT24 5BQ
☎ 01483 802903
email: hello@kosentoys.com
web: www.kosentoys.com

All Kösen's beautiful animals are made in Germany.
Company established 1912! Please email or call for
catalogue and local stockist.

● KOTO BEARS

3-25-2 Shikanodainishi, Ikoma, Nara, 630-0114,
Japan
email: kotobear@kcn.ne.jp
web: www1.kcn.ne.jp/~kotobear

Mother and daughter have been making teddy bears
professionally since around 1990.

● LAKE DISTRICT BEARS

Jacqueline Miller, 86 Springfield Avenue,
Whitehaven, Cumbria, CA28 6TT
☎ 01946 690171 mob: 07749 877233
email: lakedistrictbears@outlook.com
web: www.lakedistrictbears.co.uk

Fine quality, traditional and one of a kind collectors
bears, hand made in the Cumbrian Lake District.

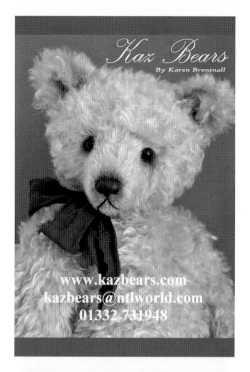

Kaz Bears
By Karen Brentnall
www.kazbears.com
kazbears@ntlworld.com
01332 731948

KOTO BEARS

3-25-2 Shikanodainishi, Ikoma, Nara, 630-0114, Japan
email: kotobear@kcn.ne.jp
web: www1.kcn.ne.jp/~kotobear
Mother and daughter have been making teddy bears
professionally since around 1990.

Lake District Bears

"A unique collection of handmade, fine quality, collectors bears"

www.lakedistrictbears.co.uk

lakedistrictbears@outlook.com

Like us on Facebook

You Tube

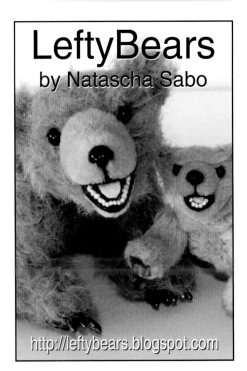

LeftyBears
by Natascha Sabo

http://leftybears.blogspot.com

LEFTY BEARS BY NATASCHA SABO

Draisstr.1, 75196 Remchingen, Germany
☎ +49 (0)7232 734812
email: natascha.sabo@t-online.de
web: http://leftybears.blogspot.com
Miniature artist bears, cats, dogs, meerkats, dragons and knitting patterns.

● ELIZABETH LEGGAT – BETH'S BEARS

Burnside, Stoneykirk, Stranraer, DG9 9EA
☎ 01776 830483 mob: 07926 626546
email: elizabeth.leggat@btinternet.com
web: www.elizabethleggat.com
Edwardian style miniature mohair teddy bears and accessories. Designed and created with the utmost attention to detail.

● LINDAL BEARS

by Linda Perkins, 267 Wellbrook Way, Girton, Cambridge, CB3 0GL
☎ 01223 277118 mob: 07803 005 965
email: lindalperkins@btinternet.com
web: www.lindalbears.com
Handmade designer mohair bears, elephants and rabbits. All one of a kind with handknitted cardigans, jumpers, hats and embellishments.

● LITTLE PIGGIES ORIGINALS

Hayley Walker
☎ 01489 896119
email: prwalker13@tiscali.co.uk
web: www.littlepiggiesnursery.com
Award winning artist creations lovingly created by Hayley using innovative designs and techniques including hand sculpting and painting. Commissions welcome.

● LITTLE SCRUFFS

8 Mill Road, Hampton, Evesham, Worcestershire, WR11 2NF
☎ mob: 07929 310275
email: littlescruffs@yahoo.co.uk
web: www.miniaturemohairbears.co.uk
'Well loved' and vintage style miniature bears, soldier bears, Fat Heads, dogs, giraffes, rabbits and other animals by Jean Grogan.

● LOGI BEARS

Maryanne Miller, 12 Hillshaw Foot, Irvine, Ayrshire, KA11 1EH
☎ 01294 213727 mob: 07790 793774
email: logibears@hotmail.com
web: www.logibears.co.uk
Hand crafted using quality fabrics, stuffed with love and care to give you a bear to treasure!

● LOLLY BOU CREATIONS

Laura Hunt, 32 Hillcroft, Dunstable, Beds, LU6 1AQ
☎ mob: 07894 526301
email: laura@lollyboucreations.co.uk
web: www.lollyboucreations.co.uk /
www.facebook.com/lollyboucreations
Bespoke hand-crafted artist mohair bears to treasure forever. Each one lovingly made with lots of character.

● LOMBARD BEARS

by Linda Down, Australia
☎ +61 (0)898 443164
email: lombardbearsaustralia@westnet.com.au
web: www.lombardbears.com
Collectable artist designed and handcrafted teddy bears, chimps and critters by Linda Down. Originality, quality and lots of character.

www.lousloveables.co.uk

Pictured are examples of
Memorial bears made from ‚left behind'
pet fleeces by Lou's Loveables

Laurent Bergmann

for LOVABLE BEARS

www.lovablebears.fr

● LOU'S LOVEABLES
email: pawsforthought@gmail.com
web: www.lousloveables.co.uk

Lou's one off bears are fully jointed and made from mohair, faux fur and 'left behind' pet fleeces.

● LOVABLE BEARS
Laurent Bergmann
☎ +33 (0)6 07718562
email: laurentbergmann@gmail.com
web: www.lovablebears.fr

I design realistic/whimsical fusion bears trying to capture the essence of realistic bears with my own sweet face designs.

● LOVE LEIGH BEARS
Walmer, Kent
email: lesleyclancy@hotmail.co.uk
web: http://loveleighbears.weebly.com

Traditional, jointed teddy bears made from mohair for the collector. Each one individual and completely hand sewn.

● MAC BEARS BY CAROL DAVIDSON
540 Rayners Lane, Pinner, Middlesex, HA5 5DJ
☎ 020 8866 4875 mob: 07904 374151
email: carolscottie@hotmail.com

Loveable hand-stitched bears, steel-shot filled.

● MADELEINE'S MINI BEARS
Madeleine Nelken, 126 Avenue du Général de Gaulle, F-78500 Sartrouville, France
☎ +33 (0)1 39 14 50 86
email: mnelken@aol.com
web: www.madeleineminibears.com

Exquisite miniature bears designed and handcrafted with love 3/4 to 5. One-offs.

● MAISI-BAEREN
Silvia Maier, Hollerwies 4, 4625 Offenhausen, Austria
☎ mob: +43 (0) 65 08 12 39 77
email: silvia_jacky@yahoo.de
web: www.maisi-baeren.de.to or www.maisi-haeltelbaaron.do.to

Crochet, as well as sewn teddies. Pure craftsmanship, only unique specimens are produced, all of which are designed by me and worked with the best materials.

● MARTI CREATES

Regina Marti, Glasgow
email: marticreates@gmail.com
web: www.marticreates.com

I create whimsical Puppen & Teddys, stitched with great joy and attention to the wonderful little details.

● MEADOWS TEDDY BEARS

42 Russell Square, Chorley, Lancashire, PR6 0AS
☎ 07845 950458
email: stephenjm1@btinternet.com

For quality and craftsmanship since 1990. Traditionally made teddy bears lovingly created in top quality mohair by Stephen J. Meadows.

● MELDRUM BEARS

Trelawn Farm, Chapel Hill, Sticker, St. Austell,
Cornwall, PL26 7HG
☎ 01726 74499 mob: 07977 422032
email: info@meldrumbears.co.uk
web: www.trelawnarts.co.uk

Handmade collectors' bears designed and created by Liz Meldrum in small limited editions. Individual commissions and special occasion bears available.

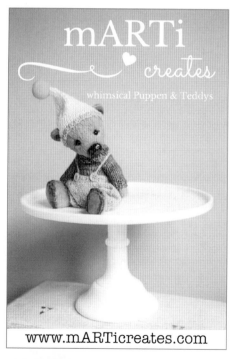

MERRYTHOUGHT LTD
Ironbridge, Telford, Shropshire, TF8 7NJ
☎ 01952 433116 Fax: 01952 432054
email: contact@merrythought.co.uk
web: www.merrythought.co.uk

The finest teddy bears: handmade in England since 1930. Traditional and limited edition designs. Exclusive projects undertaken.

MIRABEREN
Miranda Rolfes, de Lugt 2, 3043 CM, Rotterdam, Netherlands
☎ +31 (0)6305 99393
email: miraberen@gmail.com
web: http://miraberen.bearpile.com

OOAK realistic Ape and Bear designs, made from the finest fabric and materials . Commision taken

MOBY AND PUDDLE
Samantha Webb, Based in Plymouth, Devon
email: mobyandpuddle@hotmail.co.uk
web: www.mobyandpuddle.com

OOAK bears and fantasy creatures, hand sewn with love by artist Samantha Webb. Every bear has it's own tale to tell.

MONTON BEARS
Karen White, Gatewood House, Saltfleet, Lincolnshire, LN11 7RN, United Kingdom
☎ 07930 897613
email: montonbears@karenwhite456.plus.com
web: www.montonbears.com

Designer and maker of traditional & realistic bears

MUFFA MINIATURES
Mariella Vitale, Crocheted Artist Bears and Friends.
email: muffaminis@gmail.com
web: www.MuffaMiniatures.com

The smallest jointed bears ever!

MUKI BEAR – THE BEAR THAT TRAVELS
Kathy Gledhill, Purley on Thames, Reading, Berkshire, RG8 8DH
email: info@mukibear.com
web: www.mukibear.com

Jointed bear made with tweed from Yorkshire complete with canvas rucksack. Made in England. Bear to take on your travels.

Est. 1930

The Merrythought Teddy Bear
– a companion for life

Merrythought Ltd, Ironbridge, Telford, Shropshire TF8 7NJ
t: 01952 433044   e: contact@merrythought.co.uk
www.merrythought.co.uk

#merrythoughtbears

MUKI BEAR
the bear that travels

www.mukibear.com

● **MY APPLE TREE**
by Cindy Malchoff, 4131 State Route 9, Plattsburgh,
NY 12901, USA
☎ +1 518 562 4076
email: cindy@myappletree.com
web: www.myappletree.com
Handmade and designed by artist Cindy Malchoff.
Traditional style teddy bears and life-like birds.

● **NANA'S BEAR**
Sayumi Koizumi
email: 7-sayumi@krb.biglobe.ne.jp
web: www7a.biglobe.ne.jp/~nanabear/
Hand made cute mohair bears that bring a smile.

● **NESSA BEARS**
Vanessa Barham, 23 Northampton Road, Bromham,
Bedford, MK43 8QB
☎ 01234 824765 mob: 07974 818742
email: rehome@nessabears.co.uk
web: www.nessabears.co.uk
OOAK traditional vintage style bears in fine mohair,
alpaca and luxury faux fur designed and hand stitched
with love.

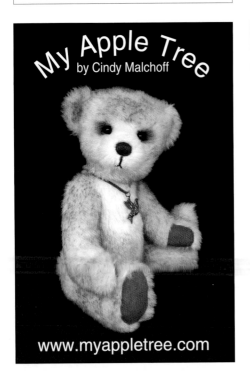

My Apple Tree
by Cindy Malchoff

www.myappletree.com

Nessa Bears

Traditional, hand-made
One of a kind teddy bears

www.nessabears.co.uk

TEDDIES FESTIVAL

Sunday, 9th September 2018

HUGGLETS
3 floors packed with bears

Twice a year Hugglets Festivals offer you over 170 stands in four bear-packed halls on three floors. Choose from 10.000 bears and related collectables on sale at each event. With four halls there's always something magical around the corner.

Kensington Town Hall Hornton Street, London

Entry: 10:30am - 4:00pm
Tickets at door: £ 4 adult,
£ 2 child

© Prue Theobalds

Parking costs £10 for 9:00am - 6:00pm (400 spaces)

Nearest Tube is High Street Kensington
Venue postcode for satnav is W8 7NX

Hugglets FESTIVALS

WMM Publishing Ltd
St James House, 13 Kensington Square
London W8 5HD, United Kingdom

Phone: +44(0)20-77 95 81 33
Email: contact@hugglets.co.uk
Internet: www.hugglets.co.uk

● NEVER JUST A BEAR

2 Fortyfoot Cottages, Pointon Fen, Sleaford,
Lincolnshire, NG34 0LF
☎ 01529 240965
email: neverjustabear@yahoo.com
web: www.neverjustabear.com

One of a kind beary folk in mohair, alpaca and luxury
faux fur. 6- 15. Collector's bears - traditional and
modern styles.

● NOWHERE BEARS

Jasmine Ivy Gladstone, The Red Door, 82 Keldgate,
Beverley, East Riding of Yorkshire, HU17 8JD
☎ mob: 07599 822478
email: jasmineivy@hotmail.co.uk
web: facebook.com/nowheretoys / instagram.com/
nowheretoys / etsy.com/uk/shop/nowheretoys

Mohair bears and other critters, handmade in Yorkshire
by award-winning bear artist Jasmine Ivy. A lot of love,
a little lunacy.

● NYXY NOOK

email: nyxynook2@gmail.com
web: www.nyxynook.xyz

Quirky, cuddly, captivating creatures by award winning
artist, Valli.

● O' LITTLE SHINE DESIGNS

Primsisters Country Decor, 8 High Street, Belper,
Derbyshire, DE56 1GF
☎ 01773 828883
email: susan.allen96666@gmail.com
web: www.etsy.com/shop/OLittleShineDesigns
Whimsical once upon a time art that bring their very
own fairytale.

● THE OLD POST OFFICE BEARS

The Old Post Office, School Lane, Twyford,
Buckinghamshire, MK18 4EY
☎ 01296 733679
email: oldpostofficebear@btinternet.com
web: www.theoldpostofficebears.com
Traditional vintage style bears designed and hand
stitched in the finest mohair by Dawn Jellis-Jones.
Specialising in miniature OOAK.

● MARINA OSETROVA

Metallurgov 62-29, Moscow, 111399, Russia
☎ mob: +7 916 8866177
email: mkingusha@gmail.com
web: www.teddy-mishka.ru
Award winning OOAK realistic bears. Custom orders
always welcome.

● OURS

Heelmeestersdreef 338, 7328KD Apeldoorn, The
Netherlands
☎ +31 (0)6 513 64684
email: judith@schnoggy.nl
web: www.schnoggy.nl
Natural miniature bears and animals, all under 4, made
to match my own photos. Also photos and photo print
shoulder bags.

● LES OURS TRICOTÉS

Anne-Dominique Thévenin, La Croix des Alouettes,
03000 Avermes, France
email: y.thevenin@free.fr
web: http://annedo.unblog.fr
Hand knitted teddies with hand made accessories,
jointed (metal rods, leather discs). Large variety of yarns
used. All my own designs.

● PADFIELD BEARS

Glossop, Derbyshire
☎ 01457 861215
email: padfieldbears@yahoo.co.uk
web: www.padfieldbears.co.uk
Michelle Doig - Making the world a furrier place.

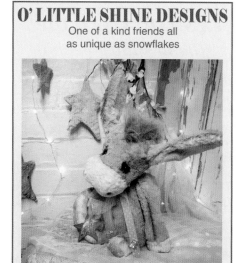

Les Ours Tricotés
(hand knitted bears)

by
Anne-Dominique
Thévenin

http://annedo.unblog.fr/

Padfield bears

www.padfieldbears.co.uk

● PAM HOWELLS
39 Frognall, Deeping St James, Peterborough, Cambridgeshire, PE6 8RR
☎ 01778 344152
Quality traditional teddy bears. Hand crafted from the finest mohair. Limited edition collectors' bears and award winning exclusive soft toys.

● PAW PRINTS OF STAFFORDSHIRE
4 Gainsmore Avenue, Norton Heights, Stoke on Trent, Staffordshire, ST6 8GE
☎ 01782 537315
email: cjkeen@pawprints.org.uk
web: www.pawprints.org.uk
Beautiful limited edition bears. Find us on Facebook: Paw Prints of Staffordshire

● PCBANGLES
79 Grenville Road, Aylesbury, Bucks, HP21 8ET
☎ mob: 07906 609831
email: pcbangles@ntlworld.com
web: www.pcbangles.uk
OOAK bears and patterns available. Mohair and hand dyed coats. All housetrained (well, most!). Come meet us online at pcBangles.

● LOUISE PEERS
2 The Lawns, Wilmslow, Cheshire, SK9 6EB
☎ 01625 527917
email: ldpeers@btinternet.com
web: www.louisepeers.blogspot.com
Award winning miniature bears. Please visit web page for available bears.

● PENNBEARY
23 Priors Walk, St Johns Priory, Lechlade, Glos, GL7 3HR
☎ 01367 252809 mob: 07519 167804
email: pennbeary@tiscali.co.uk
Award-winning mohair and Japanese silk bears. Hand stitched by Penny Roberts. Each bear is a one off edition.

● PEPPER BEARS
☎ mob: 07010 000136
email: becca@pepperbears.co.uk
web: www.pepperbears.co.uk
Hand crafted OOAK bears with character made from mohair and alpaca. Bears to collect; or commission for a unique gift.

PERTINAX BEARS

email: pertinaxbears@yahoo.co.uk
Please see display advertisement.

PIC-NIC-BEARS

Nicole Woodward
☎ mob: +33 634 95 93 32
email: ours@pic-nic-bears.com
web: www.pic-nic-bears.com

Bear artist creating original OOAK Soft Sculptures of bears & friends. Special orders, bear repairs, restoration undertaken, please contact for further info.

THE PIECE PARADE

7405 Laketree Drive, Raleigh, NC 27615, USA
☎ +1 919 870 9440
email: gbrame@pieceparade.com
web: www.pieceparade.com

Award winning teddy bears created with care and attention to detail. One-of-a-kind bears&boxes pieces.

PIPEDREAM BEARS

28 Chiltern Drive, Woodsmoor, Stockport, Cheshire, SK2 7BE
☎ 0161 285 8254
email: r.cardey@ntlworld.com
web: www.bearsandpugs.com

Handmade mohair bears by Jan Cardey and Sue Heap. Also Pipecleaner bears featuring fairies sat on handmade mushrooms.

POD BEARS

3 Ferndale Crescent, Canvey Island, Essex, SS8 0AR
☎ mob: 07492 938499
email: anita.finning@hotmail.co.uk
web: www.facebook.com/PodBears

Original artist bears and other characters created in mohair by award winning artist Anita Finning.

POGMEAR BEARS

Polmear Cottage, 8 Duporth Bay, St Austell, Cornwall
☎ mob: 07730 788581

Lovely handcrafted limited edition mohair teddy bears and friends for collectors by Jacqueline Wright.

PRIMROSE COTTAGE BEARS

Valerie Simpson
☎ 0176 0440809
email: primcottbears@yahoo.co.uk
web: www.primrosecottagebears.co.uk

Limited Edition and one of a kind mohair collector's bears and hares, hand made with love for you to treasure.

Email: pertinaxbears@yahoo.co.uk

Pipedream Bears

tel 0161 2858254
Mobile 07905766899
r.cardey@ntlworld.com
www.bearsandpugs.com

● PUMPKIN & PICKLE BEARS
East Sussex
☎ 01892 652706
email: pumpkinandpickle@hotmail.co.uk
web: www.pumpkinandpickle.co.uk
OOAK bears made by award winning artist Gemma McKenzie.

● PUZZLE BEARS
61 Send Road, Send, Nr Woking, Surrey, GU23 7EU
☎ **01483 224524**
email: **puzzlebears@hotmail.co.uk**
web: **www.puzzlebears.bearpile.com**
Handmade collectors bears and animals, designed by Anita Weller. Traditional, themed character and miniature bears made to order.

● QUE-SERA BEARS
Que-Sera, 169 Bures Road, Gt. Cornard, Sudbury, Suffolk, CO10 0JG
☎ 01787 375575 mob: 07814 232317
email: noy2002@talktalk.net
Mohair bears in crocheted outfits or just bear, made in the heart of Suffolk, just waiting for a cuddle.

● THE RABBIT MAKER
email: shelly@therabbitmaker.com
web: www.therabbitmaker.com
Shelly Allison is an award winning soft sculpture artist. Her rabbits have fine costuming and lots of character. See photo in the Gallery.

● RUBEN BEARS
164 Cutenhoe Road, Luton, Bedfordshire, LU1 3NF
☎ 01582 731544
email: rubenbears@aol.com
Lovable bears requiring loving homes.

● SACQUE BEARS
by Susan Anne Coulthard, Ebenezer House, Roes Lane, Crich, Derbyshire, DE4 5DH
☎ 01773 853159
email: sacquebears@aol.comor sacoulthard@aol.com
Award winning bears. Handmade limited edition and commission bears available direct or through selected stockists. Enquiries welcome.

SALLY B GOLLIES

12 Bridges Close, Wokingham, Berks, RG41 3XL
☎ 0118 9775464 Fax: 0118 9773228
email: zarir@btinternet.com

Distinctive, individual gollies often with subjects of well
known characters from stage, screen or history. Always
depicted kindly and humorously.

SAMANTHA-JANE BEARS

31 Gloucestershire Lea, Warfield, Bracknell,
Berkshire, RG42 3XQ
☎ 01344 443748
email: samanthajanebears@outlook.com
web: www.samantha-janebears.co.uk

Beautiful original bears and scallycat kittens designed
and crafted by award winning artist Samantha-jane
Seeley since 1997.

SAMT AND ROSES BÄREN

Ika Wagner-Heinze, Dammstrasse 69,
33824 Werther , Germany
☎ +49 5203 5605 mob: 0049 151 5608 9789
email: ika.wagner.heinze@googlemail.com
web: www.samtandrosesbaeren.jimdo.com

Sometimes it needs all day to get the expression of the
faces. I want to look them kind and lovely.

SANDRAS BÄRENBANDE ...DIE MIT DEN ROSEN

Sandra Kunz, Rodheimer Straße 59,
35633 Lahnau, Germany
email: info@sandras-baerenbande.de
web: www.sandras-baerenbande.info

Hand sewn teddy bears and other animals made in high
quality antique style mohair with rose-printed footpads.

SCRUFFIE BEARS BY SUSAN PRYCE

19 Parkfield Road, Broughton, Nr Chester,
Flintshire, CH4 0SE
☎ 01244 534724
email: scruffiebears@aol.com
web: www.scruffiebears.com

Beautiful teddy bears created from mohair or luxurious
faux fur by an award winning artist.

SHANTOCK BEARS

14 Southend Lane, Northall, Dunstable, Beds, LU6 2EX
☎ 01525 794081 mob: 07762 749104
email: shantockbears@outlook.com
web: www.shantockbears.com

Award winning bears and friends by Elanor. Hand knitted
clothes by Lyn.

www.samtandrosesbaeren.jimdo.com

Samt and Roses Bären

Sandras Bärenbande...
... die mit den Rosen

Sandra Kunz

www.sandras-baerenbande.info

Shantock Bears

www.shantockbears.com
01525 794081

Shebob Bears
by Sheila Tester
tel: 01535 652072
sheila.tester@tesco.net

● SHEBOB BEARS
73 Thornhill Road, Steeton, Keighley, Yorkshire,
BD20 6RE
☎ 01535 652072
email: sheila.tester@tesco.net
Loveable, individually handcrafted bears and other
critters with personality and style, created for the most
discerning collector. See Gallery picture.

● JULIE SHEPHERD
☎ 01730 810878
email: julie@julieshepherd.com
web: www.julieshepherd.com
Bears, bunnies and pandas with kind and gentle faces.
Designed and lovingly crafted by award winning artist.
Photos available.

● SHULTZ CHARACTERS
by Paula Strethill-Smith
☎ 01329 834681 Fax: As tel.
email: info@paulastrethill-smith.com
web: www.paulastrethill-smith.com /
www.paulastrethill-smith.blogspot.co.uk
Created by Paula Strethill-Smith, international award
winning artist. Vintage style miniature teddy bears, dogs,
mice, rabbits and other characters.

● ELENA STANILEVICI
str. Renasterii 3, com. Stauceni, mun. Chisinau,
MD-2050, Moldova
☎ +373 783-05-555
email: teddydoll.se@gmail.com
web: https://elenastanilevici.bearpile.com
Teddy and doll artist. OOAK bears and animals. Hand
stitched, full of character and personality. My Facebook
page: www.facebook.com/stanilevici

● STEEL CITY BEARS
The Bear Emporium
email: bears@bear-emporium.com
web: www.bear-emporium.com
Handcrafted plush and OOAK mohair and alpaca
bears, lovingly made in Sheffield. Many named on
Sheffield theme.

● STEIFF UK
Astra House, The Common, Cranleigh, Surrey,
GU6 8RZ
☎ +44 (0)1483 266643 Fax: +44 (0)1483 266646
email: leyla.maniera@steiff.com
web: www.steiff.com
Visit www.steiff-club.de to find your nearest stockist.

● STRAWBEARY DESIGNS

Helen Mawson, 27 Windermere Road, Carnforth, Lancashire, LA5 9AR
☎ 01524 733862 mob: 07917 798415
email: strawbeary_designs@yahoo.co.uk
web: www.strawbearydesigns.co.uk

Bespoke collectable bears and bunnys. Traditionally jointed and hand crafted with love. Made using the finest Mohair and other quality fabrics.

● STREETEBEARS

Sue Streete, 86, School Road, Copford, Colchester, Essex, CO6 1BX
☎ 01206 210457 mob: 07391589722
email: susan.streete@gmail.com

Collector Bears designed and handmade by Sue. Steampunk, Historical and Tradional.can be made to order e-mail for details.

● SUE'S TEDS

Sue Powell, Hampton Lovett, Droitwich, Worcester
☎ 01905 554569 mob: 07914 218341
email: suesteds@sky.com
web: www.sues-teds.co.uk

Individual hand made mohair and alpaca bears and bunnies by Sue Powell. Happy and smiling and made with love.

Sue Thomas
email: hello@tedandsue.co
www.tedandsue.co

Teddies Garden

Artist bears by
Katherine Uphill

www.teddiesgarden.co.uk

● **SWEENIKLE BEARS**
by Natalie Standing
email: sweeniklebears@gmail.com
web: www.sweeniklebears.co.uk
One of a kind, hand made artist bears with irresistible
faces, bringing together the best tradition and modern.

● **SYLVI BEARS**
Sylvia Smith, Isle of Wight
email: sylvi-bears@hotmail.com
web: www.facebook.com/sylvi.bears1
Every Bear unique with its own personality, just waiting
patiently for a new home and family to love them.

● **TEDANDSUE**
Sue Thomas, Ware Barn, Ware Lane, Lyme Regis,
Devon, DT7 3RH
☎ mob: 07887 511774
email: hello@tedandsue.co
web: www.TedandSue.co
Bears, Bunnies & Imagination

● **TEDDIES GARDEN**
Katherine Uphill, Flat 29 Chester House, Imperial
Road, Exmouth, Devon, EX8 1DB
☎ 01395 267359 mob: 07456 788987
email: info@teddiesgarden.co.uk
web: www.teddiesgarden.co.uk
Beautiful bears created from the finest quality materials
by Katherine Uphill using traditional bear-crafting and
floral art techniques.

● **TEDDY BEAR ARTISTS AND
FRIENDS**
Administrators: Mohair Bear Making Supplies,
Worldwide online community
email: tbaaf.online@virginmedia.com
web: www.teddy-bear-artists-and-friends.com
A collectors paradise! Enter the Annual TBAAF Awards!
View 1000s of bears and dolls for sale direct from the
artists!

● **TEDDY ECKE**
Martina Lehr, Grosse Gasse 4a, 64720 Michelstadt,
Germany
☎ +40 (0) 60 61 04 08 09
email: info@teddy-ecke.de
web: www.teddy-ecke.de
Simply enchanting and hand made with love for details
- bears and animals from hand coloured fabrics made
by Martina Lehr.

● TEDS FROM THE TYNE
Gillian Wilkinson, 21 Northmoor Road, Newcastle upon Tyne, NE6 4RY
☎ 0191 2621 659
email: gillysbears@sky.com
web: www.facebook.com/tedsfromthetyne
Traditional bears, superbly crafted using the finest materials. Original designs created in the heart of the North East.

● TEENY BEARS
11 Sparsholt Road, Weston, Southampton, Hants, SO19 9NH
☎ 02380 446356
email: tina@teenybears.co.uk
web: www.teenybears.co.uk
Teddy Bears, Gollys and cupcakes designed and hand made with love by Tina. Please look at my website for details.

● TELLYBEARS
Estelle Lichtenberger-Froehling, 13, rue Kiem, Gonderange, Luxembourg
email: estelle.lichtenberger@gms.lu
web: www.tellybears.net
Handcrafted vintage & classic teddybears from Luxembourg by Estelle Lichtenberger-Froehling.

● THE THING ABOUT BEARS

Sam Glanville, The Olde Bear Workshop, 163 Mongeham Road. Great Mongeham. Deal. Kent. CT14 9LL
☎ mob: 07769 325932
email: thingaboutbears@aol.com
web: www.thethingaboutbears.com
Quality hand crafted artist bears, made with love. Weekly evening bear making classes in Deal, Kent. Day classes also held.

● THREADTEDS

De Braak 11, 5963 BA Horst, The Netherlands
☎ +31 (0)77 3984960
email: threadteds@xs4all.nl
web: www.threadteds.com

Collectible Thread Artist Bears and Friends. Patterns and supplies. Specializing in long, X-long and new!! -XX long pile mini bear fabrics.

● TICKETY BOO BEARS

Folkestone, Kent
☎ mob: 0774 786 7523
email: ticketyboo-bears@hotmail.co.uk
web: www.facebook.com/Ticketyboobears

Bears to make you smile. Designed and handstitched by Paula Stammers. Enquiries always welcome.

● TONNIBEARS

by Marjan Balke, Brauergildenstrasse 17, 38300 Wolfenbüttel, Germany
email: bears@tonnibears.nl
web: www.tonnibears.nl

Dutch artist living in Germany celebrating her 25th year of award winning one-of-a kind and small edition bears and other critters.

● TOYS, STUFFED AND HANDMADE BY SUSAN

23 Sabrina Drive, Toronto, Ontario, M9R 2J4, Canada
☎ +1 416 242 6446
email: smansfield.jones@gmail.com
Soft: A variety of fabrics both Faux and Mohair. Stuffed: Variety of Animals. Sculpture: From 4 inches – 4 feet (Commissions allow 4 weeks)

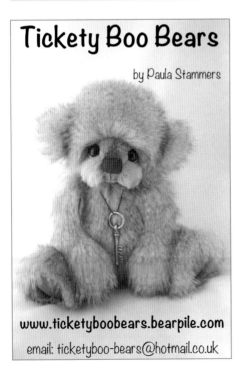

● TRACIE BEARS

3 High Howe Close, Bournemouth, Dorset, BH11 8NN
☎ 0330 088 3993
email: enquiries@traciebears.co.uk
web: www.traciebears.co.uk
Loveable handmade bears in a variety of fabrics. Characters
and specials available. Commissions and visitors welcome.

● TWEEDIES

Orchard House, Church Lane, Orleton, Ludlow,
Shropshire, SY8 4HU
☎ 01568 780479 mob: 07917 264237
email: patricia@tweedies.biz Fax: 01568 780961
web: www.tweedies.biz
13 years of award winning original and colourful
Shetland and Welsh tweed bears and paperweight mice.
All handcrafted with love.

● VALEWOOD BEARS

17 Belmont Gardens, Lowestoft, Suffolk, NR32 4EJ
☎ 01502 562783
email: pwdesigns44@gmail.com
web: www.valewoodbears.com
Individually hand crafted, unique mohair bears and
bunnies. Also exquisite hand made teddy bear clothes.

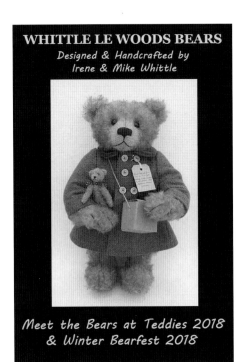

WHITTLE LE WOODS BEARS
*Designed & Handcrafted by
Irene & Mike Whittle*

*Meet the Bears at Teddies 2018
& Winter Bearfest 2018*

● VINTAGEDECO BEARS

The Netherlands
email: vdbears@outlook.com
web: www.vintagedecobears.com /
www.facebook.com/VintageDecoBears /
www.bear.center/artists/vintagedeco-bears/creations

'Traditional Vintage Style' collector bears with individual
characters. Handcrafted, fully jointed and filled with
woodwool or sawdust.

● WACKY WALKER BEARS

by Liz Walker Watts, 16 Titchfield Close, Grange
Park, Swindon, Wiltshire, SN5 6HS
☎ mob: +44 7851724432
email: lizwalkerwatts@btinternet.com
web: www.facebook.com/wackywalker.bears /
http://wackywalkerbears.bearpile.com

A self-taught mixed media artist creating unique individuals
for 20+ years from 'Wacky' to whimsical or just darn cute.

● WARRENS BEAR PATCH & MAGICAL REALMS

Rob & Caz
☎ mob: 07803 807584
email: warrensbearpatch@gmail.com
web: www.warrensbearpatchandmagicalrealms.co.uk

Artist Teddy Bears, Reborn Babies, Teddy Bear Friends
and much more....

● WEE BEARY TAILS BEARS

24 Hunters Forstal Road, Broomfield, Herne Bay,
Kent, CT6 7DN
☎ 01227 741352 Fax: As tel.
email: beary_tails@yahoo.co.uk
web: www.weebearytailsbears.com and
www.facebook.com/Wee-Beary-Tails-Bears-
191353080997149

Contemporary, colourful, creative, OOAK, handmade
mohair artist bears & critters by Rachel Summersby -
created with love, sending smiles Worldwide!

● WHITTLE-LE-WOODS BEARS

23 Leinster Street, Farnworth, Bolton, Lancashire,
BL4 9HS
☎ 01204 706831
email: wlwbears@gmail.com
web: www.wlwbears.co.uk

Collectable Artist Teddy Bears, see our latest designs on
our new website address launching soon.

● THE WILD THINGS

Susan Donaj, Im Spring 25, 45739 Oer-
Erkenschwick, Germany
☎ +49 (0)2368 56165
email: sushi.2@t-online.de
web: www.sushis-wild-thing.com

Sweet bears made and designed by Susan Donaj. Watch
my website for regular updates please.

● WOODLAND TEDDIES

Rita Simmonds, 5 Mildenhall Road, Loughborough,
Leicestershire, LE11 4SN
☎ 01509 267597 mob: 07973 821816
email: rita@woodlandteddies.com or .co.uk
web: www.woodlandteddies.com /
www.woodlandteddies.co.uk

Innovative, award winning artist designing and creating
superbly realistic to wildly OTT critters that are handsewn, handdyed and deliciously original.

END

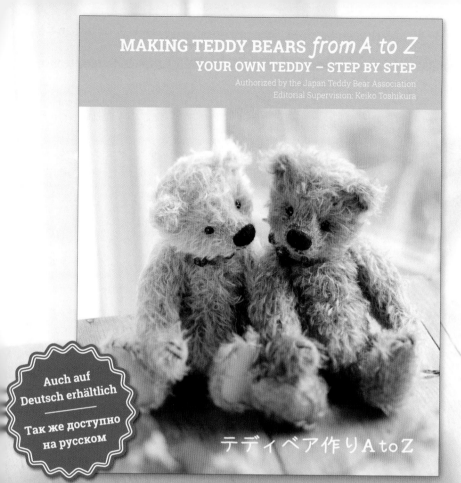
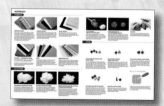 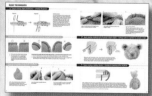 

Website Index

Bears To Collect — www.bears2collect.co.uk
BEARS UPON SOAR — www.bearsuponsoar.co.uk
Bears&Buds Online Monthly Teddy Bear Magazine — www.bearsandbuds.com
bears2hares — www.facebook.com/Bears2hares
BeauT Bears — www.beautbears.nl
Bebbin Bears — www.bebbinbears.co.uk
Bebesandbruins.com — www.bebesandbruins.com
Bello Born Bears — www.bellobornbears.com
Benson Bears — www.bensonbears.com
BERTIE SWEEDLEPIPE BEARS — www.BertieSweedlepipeBears.bearpile.com
Bisson Bears — www.bissonbears.co.uk
Black Mountain Bears — www.blackmountainbears.co.uk
Blakesley Bears Ltd — www.blakesleybears.com
Blee Bears — www.bleebears.co.uk
Blinko Bears — www.blinkobears.co.uk
Bobby's Bears — www.facebook.com/bobbysbears
Bourton Bears — www.bourtonbears.com
Bow Gussies — www.bowgussies.bearpile.com
BowerBird Bears — www.bowerbirdbears.co.uk
Bradgate Bears — www.bradgatebears.co.uk
Brewins' Bruins — www.brewinsbruins.co.uk
Brierley Bears — www.brierleybears.co.uk
Bright Star Teddy Bear Shows Online — www.bright-star-promotions.com
Britannia Bears — www.britanniabears.co.uk
The British Bear Collection — www.thebritishbearcollection.co.uk
Brotherwood Bears — www.brotherwoodbears.com
BSB Bear Supplies — www.stores.ebay.co.uk/bsb-bear-supplies
Bumble Bears — www.bumble—bears.com
Bumbly Bears — www.bumblybears.co.uk
Bygone Bears — www.bygone—bears.com
C&T Auctions — www.candtauctions.co.uk
Cama-Baeren — www.camabaeren.de
CarroBears — www.facebook.com/CarroBears
Caterham Yesterbears — http://yesterbears.blogspot.co.uk
Cejais Bears & Dollshouses — www.cejais.net
Charlie Bears Limited — www.charliebears.com
Chatham Village Bears L.L.C. — www.chathamvillagebears.com
Cheltenham Bears — www.cheltenhambears.co.uk
The Chocolate Box — www.chocolateandbears.com
Christie Bears Limited — www.christiebears.com
Christopher's Chairs — www.christopherschairs.co.uk
Claudinours — www.claudinours.sitew.com
Clemens Bears of Germany — www.clemens-spieltiere.de
Clumsy Bears — www.clumsybears.co.uk
CodeName Butterfly — www.codenamebutterfly.com
Collector Button Bears — www.collectorbuttonbears.co.uk
Conradi Creations — www.conradicreations.com
Corfe Bears — www.corfebears.co.uk
Cornwall Bear Fairs — www.urchinsbears.com
Cowslip Bear Company — www.cowslipbears.co.uk

The Creative Tedd — www.thecreativetedd.co.uk
Cuddlekin Bears — www.cuddlekinbears.co.uk
Cupboard Bears — http://cupboardbears.blogspot.co.uk
D and A Bears — www.dandabears.uk
Dandelion Bear Orphans — www.dandelionbears.bearpile.com
Dari Laut Bears — www.dari-laut-bears.co.uk
Deb Canham Artist Designs — www.debcanham.com
Doll & Teddy Fairs — www.dollandteddyfairs.co.uk
Dolls, Bears and Bygones — www.dollsbearsandbygones.co.uk
Dolly's Daydreams — www.dollysdaydreams.com
Dreli-Bears & Dragons — www.mazzitelli.at
DS-BÄREN — www.ds-baeren.de
Earth Angels Studios — www.EarthAngelsStudios.com
EcoBears — www.ecobears.com
Edenbears — www.edenbears.co.uk
Elena Stanilevici — https://elenastanilevici.bearpile.com
Elle et L'Ours — www.elleetlours.jimdo.com
Everyn Rose — www.facebook.com/masako.kitao
Fantasia Textiles — www.fantasiatextiles.co.uk
Flopsey Bears — www.flopseybears.com
Flutter-By Bears — www.flutter-by-bears.co.uk
Frou-Frou — www.frou-froubears.com
Futch Bears — www.futchbears.co.uk
Fuzzies Fluff n Stuff — www.fuzziesfluffnstuff.co.uk
G & T Evans Woodwool — www.gtevans.co.uk
GarJar Bears — garjarbears.wixsite.com/garjarbears
Gill Dobson Teddy Bears — www.gilldobsonteddybears.co.uk
Gold Teddy Bears — www.goldteddy.co.uk
GOLDEN GEORGE — www.golden-george.com
Grange Hollow — www.grangehollow.com
The Great Teddy Bear Events Company — www.thegreatyorkshireteddybearevent.co.uk
Gyll's Bears — www.gyllsbears.bearpile.com
Haja-Bears — www.haja-bears.com
Hand Glass Craft — www.handglasscraft.com
Handmade Keepsake Rag Dolls and Collectables — www.facebook.com/HandmadeKeepsakeRagDollsandcollectables
Hansa Creation Inc. — www.hansa-uk.com
Haven Bears — www.havenbears.co.uk
A Helmbold GmbH — www.A-Helmbold.de
Hermann Teddy Original — www.teddy-hermann.de
Hidden Cove Bears — www.hiddencovebears.co.uk
Higgys Bears — www.higgysbears.co.uk
Hollinfare Bears — www.hollinfarebears.webs.com
HONEYDEW BEARS — www.honeydewbears.co.za
Hugglets — www.hugglets.co.uk
Huggy Bears UK — www.facebook.com/HuggyBearsUK
Hugoshouse — www.hugoshouse.com
Huwi Bears — www.Huwibears.ch
JCW Bears & Furry Friends — www.jcwbears.co.uk
JEKABAER — www.jekabaer.de
Jenni Bears — www.jennibears.co.uk

Jinnee Bears of Exeter — www.jinneebearsofexeter.co.uk

Joxy Bears — www.joxybears.com

Ju-Beary Bears — www.jubearybears.com

JUST BEARS UK — www.justbearsuk.co.uk

K.M. Bears — www.kmbears.co.uk

KALEideaSCOPE — www.kaleideascope.net

KAREN ALDERSON ARTIST DESIGN — www.karenalderson.com/bears

KatieCountryBears — www.katiecountrybears.co.uk

KayAnne Kreations — www.kayannekreations.co.uk

Kaycee Bears™ — www.kayceebears.co.uk

Kaytkins Bears — www.facebook.com/kaytkins.bears

Kaz Bears — www.kazbears.com

Kevinton Bears — www.kevintonbears.com

Kieron James Toys — www.kieronjamestoys.co.uk

Kingswear Bears and Friends — www.kingswearbears.com

Knockie Bears by Slackstitches — www.slackstitches.com

Koko's Bear Shop — www.kokosbearshop.com

Kösen UK — www.kosentoys.com

Koto Bears — www1.kcn.ne.jp/~kotobear

La Mode Pour Les Ours — www.lamodepourlesours.co.uk

Lake District Bears — www.lakedistrictbears.co.uk

Lefty Bears by Natascha Sabo — http://leftybears.blogspot.com

Elizabeth Leggat – Beth's Bears — www.elizabethleggat.com

Lindal Bears — www.lindalbears.com

Little Piggies Originals — www.littlepiggiesnursery.com

Little Scruffs — www.miniaturemohairbears.co.uk

Logi Bears — www.logibears.co.uk

Lolly Bou Creations — www.lollyboucreations.co.uk

Lombard Bears — www.lombardbears.com

London International Antique Doll, Teddy Bear and Toy Fair — www.200yearsofchildhood.com

Lou's Loveables — www.lousloveables.co.uk

Lovable Bears — www.lovablebears.fr

Love Leigh Bears — http://loveleighbears.weebly.com

Madeleine's Mini Bears — www.madeleineminibears.com

Magpies Gifts Ltd — www.charliebearsuk.com

Maisi-Baeren — www.maisi-baeren.de.to

mARTi creates — www.marticreates.com

Meldrum Bears — www.trelawnarts.co.uk

Merrythought Ltd — www.merrythought.co.uk

Miraberen — http://miraberen.bearpile.com

Moby and Puddle — www.mobyandpuddle.com

Mohair Bear Making Supplies — www.mohairbearmakingsupplies.co.uk

Monton Bears — www.montonbears.com

Morpheus Wilson — www.facebook.com/MorpheusWilsonVintage

Muffa Miniatures — www.MuffaMiniatures.com

MUKI BEAR – THE BEAR THAT TRAVELS — www.mukibear.com

Mumbles — www.the-mumbles.co.uk

My Apple Tree — www.myappletree.com

Nana's Bear — www7a.biglobe.ne.jp/~nanabear/

Nessa Bears — www.nessabears.co.uk

Bear Business Phone Directory

A

A bear named Jack. 07788 874888

Abbey Bears. 01841 532484

Abby's Bears . . . . +27 (0)72387 0576

ABC ~ Tedi Bach Hug / Dreamtime . . 01952 270023

Abracadabra Teddy Bears 01799 527222

All Bear by Paula Carter. 01622 686970

All Things Beary 0131 477 6970

Ann Made Bears. 01837 849063

Arctophilia 01952 604096

Art Doll Expo. . . . . +86 136 019 20831

The Artful Bear 01383 824306

Ashby Bears. 01530 564444

Asquiths World Famous Teddy Bear Shop. . . . .

. . . . 01491 571978

Atelier WiBa-Bär. . . . . +49 (0)2371 29845

Atique & Urchins Bears 01840 779009

Aurorabearealis 01463 731110

B

B's Bears 07788 755882

Ba's Bears 01865 435314

Baby Talk Bears by Soyo . . . . +81 80 4422 7692

Bacton Bears 01449 781087

Bakewell Gift & Bear Shop. 01629 814811

Barbara-Ann Bears 01303 870087

Bärenstübchen Blümmel . . . . . . +49 (0)621 4838812

Barling Bears 01732 845059

Barrel Bears 07974 994302

Barron Bears . . . . +1 760 598 9123

Bear Basics 01963 34500

Bear Bits . . . . please see website

Bear Essentials. . . . . +353 (0)49 9523461

BEAR GALLERY. 028 2588 2262

The Bear Garden. 01483 302581

Bear It In Mind 07867 787795

The Bear Necessities – Knarf-Bears . +32 (0)5034 1027

Bear Rhymes 07513645009

The Bear Shop 01603 766866

Bear Workshops By The Sea 01303 870087

Bearable Bears. . . . . +31 (0)55 5788067

Bearleigh Bears . . . . +61 (0)4 3801 6714

Bearlytherehugs 01388 602550

Bearmore Bears 07849 001528

Bears ‚N' Company. . . . . +1 647 351 6427

Bears at the Vale 0207 328 2280

Bears by Karen. 07783 474259

Bears by Sue Quinn 0141 887 9916

Bears by Susan Jane Knock. 01376 521230

Bears on the Square 01952 433924

Bears To Collect 01480 860376

BEARS UPON SOAR 07866 616799

Bears&Buds Online Monthly Teddy Bear Magazine . . .

. . . . +1 502 423 7827

bears2hares. 07513 538807

Beatrix Bears 01743 340276

BeauT Bears. . . . . +31 (0)610 623 559

Bebbin Bears 01296 423755

Bebes et Jouets 01289 304802

Bell Bears. 020 8778 0217

Bello Born Bears. 001-714-719 10 84

Benson Bears. . . . . +61 (0)3 639 66150

BERTIE SWEEDLEPIPE BEARS 07854 359555

Dot Bird 01765 607131

Bisson Bears 0047 47834123

Blakesley Bears Ltd. 01865 600587

Blee Bears 01295 258535

Blinko Bears 07799 660962

Bobby's Bears 01204 468090

Bourton Bears. 01452 700608

Bow Gussies. 01905 312304

BowerBird Bears. 07979 595397

Bradgate Bears. 0116 236 7147

Brewins' Bruins 01929 761398

Bridgwater Bears 01473 412066

Brierley Bears. 01226 714674

Bright Star Teddy Bear Shows Online +1 502 423 7827

Britannia Bears. 01945 475197

The British Bear Collection. . . 01934 822263/822342

Brotherwood Bears 01249 322300

BSB Bear Supplies 01752 403515

Bumble Bears. 02380 326663

Bumbly Bears. 01639 813514

Burlington Bearties 01384 279731

Bygone Bears 01202 739926

C

C&T Auctions 07736 668702

CarroBears. . . . . +46 (0)70 320 22 62

Caterham Yesterbears. 01883 346107

Cejais Bears & Dollshouses 024 76 633630

Charlie Bears Limited 01566 777092

Chatham Village Bears L.L.C.. . . . . +1 314 566 2940

Cheltenham Bears 07905 307859

The Chocolate Box 01484 688222

Christie Bears Limited 01656 670372

Christopher's Chairs 01425 475662

Claudinours . . . . +33 (0)325 324 706

Clemens Bears of Germany 01246 269723

Clumsy Bears 07789 392235

CodeName Butterfly 07341 656302

Conradi Creations 07576685143

Corfe Bears 01929 426827

Cornwall Bear Fairs. 01840 779009

Cowslip Bear Company 01202 382073

The Creative Tedd. 07859 001340

Crotchety Bears 01562 752289

Cuddlekin Bears 07930 247948

Cupboard Bears 01425 838342

D

D and A Bears 07803 092563

Dandelion Bear Orphans 07526 500182

Dari Laut Bears. 01424 754418

Doll & Teddy Fairs. 07973 760881

Dolls, Bears and Bygones 07889 630051

Dolly's Daydreams 01945 870160

Dreli-Bears & Dragons. . . . . . . +43 (0)664 412 4671

DS-BÄREN 00 49/63 21 597 35

DuBears. 01773 590668

E

Earth Angels Studios. . . . . +1 845 986 8720

EcoBears 00 44 (0) 7486860899

Elena Stanilevici . . . . +373 783-05-555

Elle et L'Ours . . . . +33 688 312591

Elliebears 01268 762438

Everyn Rose . . . . +81 (0)436 22 6823

F

Fantasia Textiles. 01787 222946

Flopsey Bears. 07818 037662

Flutter-By Bears 01782 560136

Frou-Frou. 01543 426661

Futch Bears 07930 335192

Fuzzies Fluff n Stuff. . . . . 01706 372562 option 4

G

G & T Evans Woodwool 01686 622100

Gill Dobson Teddy Bears 01347823122

Gold Teddy Bears 01924 420272

Golden George . . . . +49 (0)404291 77100

Grange Hollow 01634 570331

The Great Teddy Bear Events Company. 07852 937518

Jo Greeno. 01483 224312

Gyll's Bears 020 8366 1836

H

Haja-Bears . . . . +31 (0)318 619103
Hand Glass Craft. 01384 573410
Handmade Keepsake Rag Dolls and Collectables . . . .
. . . . 07432 732691
Hansa Creation Inc. 020 8954 5956
Hardy Bears 01305 835435
Haven Bears. 07948 200031
A Helmbold GmbH. . . . . +49 (0)3764 188090
Hermann Teddy Original . . . . . . +49 (0)9543 84820
Hidden Cove Bears 01626 853251
Higgys Bears 01323 841819
Hoblins. 01772 635516
Hollinfare Bears 07708 983895
Holly Bears 01889 568848
HONEYDEW BEARS. . . . . +27 (0)11 764 4317
Hovvigs . . . . +45 5991 3494
Pam Howells. 01778 344152
Huggy Bears UK 01623 458514
Hugoshouse 01932 243263
Huwi Bears. 0041 79 453 19 61

J

Jan's Tiddy Bears 07889 794637
JCW Bears & Furry Friends 01268 726558
JEKABAER 00 49/151/21 73 97 87
Jenni Bears 01625 877184
Jinnee Bears of Exeter. 01392 257315
Jodie's Bears . . . . +81 (0)466 25 1202
Joxy Bears 01262 679688
Ju-Beary Bears. 07711 191241
JUST BEARS UK 07736 320011

K

K.M. Bears 0113 2299 899
KALEideaSCOPE . . . . +41 (0)61 8310444
Natasha Kataeva. . . . . +7 342 216 74 75
KatieCountryBears 01524 823558
KayAnne Kreations 01782 912957

Kaycee Bears™ 01507 363955
Kaysbears by Kay Street 01474 351757
Kaytkins Bears 01933 355782
Kaz Bears. 01332 731948
Kieron James Toys 01444 484870
Kingswear Bears and Friends. 01803 752632
Knockie Bears by Slackstitches 01542 840551
Koko's Bear Shop 01983 616815
Kösen UK 01483 802903

L

La Mode Pour Les Ours. 07712 660582
Lake District Bears 01946 690171
Lefty Bears by Natascha Sabo . . +49 (0)7232 734812
Elizabeth Leggat – Beth's Bears. 01776 830483
Reinhold Lesch GmbH. 020 7794 2377
Lindal Bears. 01223 277118
Little Piggies Originals. 01489 896119
Little Scruffs. 07929 310275
Logi Bears 01294 213727
Lolly Bou Creations 07894 526301
Lombard Bears. . . . . +61 (0)898 443164
London International Antique Doll, Teddy Bear and Toy Fair
. . . . 07875 874854
Lovable Bears. . . . . +33 (0)6 07718562

M

Mac Bears by Carol Davidson 020 8866 4875
Madeleine's Mini Bears . . . . . . +33 (0)1 39 14 50 86
Magpies Gifts Ltd 01626 353456
Maisi-Baeren . . . . +43 (0) 65 08 12 39 77
Meadows Teddy Bears 07845 950458
Meldrum Bears. 01726 74499
Merrythought Ltd 01952 433116
Miraberen . . . . +31 (0)6305 99393
Mohair Bear Making Supplies 01952 604096
Monton Bears. 07930 897613
Morpheus Wilson 07548 120977
Mumbles 01506 437226
My Apple Tree . . . . +1 518 562 4076

N

Nessa Bears 01234 824765
Never Just a Bear 01529 240965
Norbeary Fabrics 01303 870087
Nowhere Bears 07599 822478

O

O' Little Shine Designs 01773 828883
The Old Bear Company 01246 850117
Old Bears Lodge 01443 776031
Old Bears Network 01422 823079
The Old Post Office Bears 01296 733679
Old Teddy Bear Shop 01404 823444
Olga Arkhipova . . . . +79151359778
Once Upon A Time Bears 01377 236621
The Optimists 07769 157406
Marina Osetrova . . . . +7 916 8866177
OURS . . . . +31 (0)6 513 64684

P

Padfield Bears 01457 861215
Pat Rush 01743 231457
Paw Prints of Staffordshire 01782 537315
Paws in the Forest 02380 282697
pcbangles 07906 609831
Peacock Fibres Ltd 01274 633900
Sue Pearson 01273 595734
Louise Peers 01625 527917
Pennbeary 01367 252809
Pepper Bears 07816 398135
pic-nic-bears . . . . +33 634 95 93 32
The Piece Parade . . . . +1 919 870 9440
Pipedream Bears 0161 285 8254
Pod Bears 07492 938499
Pogmear Bears 07730 788581
Poli Plastic Pellets Ltd 01244 940973
Primrose Cottage Bears 0176 0440809
Pumpkin & Pickle Bears 01892 652706
Puzzle Bears 01483 224524

Q

Que-Sera Bears 01787 375575

R

Ruben Bears 01582 731544

S

Sacque Bears 01773 853159
Sally B Gollies 0118 9775464
Samantha-jane Bears 01344 443748
SAMT AND ROSES BÄREN 0049 5203 5605
Scruffie Bears by Susan Pryce 01244 534724
Serendipity 01422 340097
Shantock Bears 01525 794081
Shebob Bears 01535 652072
Julie Shepherd 01730 810878
Mary Shortle . . . . 01132 456160 / 452 005
Shultz Characters 01329 834681
Smiffy Bears 07885 075890
Sophy Labbett 01293 862760
Special Auction Services 01635 580595
Spielzeug Welten Museum Basel . +41 (0)61 225 95 95
St Martin's Gallery 01425 489090
Steiff UK . . . . +44 (0)1483 266643
Stonebow Bears 01522 529219
StrawBeary Designs 01524 733862
Streetebears 01206 210457
Sue's Teds 01905 554569
Sunny Vintage & Retro and Teddy Hospital 07426 251117
Sylvi Bears 07826 308447

T

TABBYCLOUDS 07858 926591
TedandSue 07887 511774
Teddies Garden 01395 267359
TEDDY BEAR ATTIC UK 01981 241062
The Teddy Bear Museum Shop 01305 266040
The Teddy Bear Museum 01305 266040
Teddy Bear Paintings 01664 851314
Teddy Bears of Witney 01993 706616

Teddy Bears' Picknick . . . . +31 (0)343 577068

Teddy Boutique 01756 709676

Teddy Ecke 00 49 (0) 60 61 94 98 09

Teddy Station 01702 611106

TeddyBär Total . . . . +49 (0)404291 77100

Teddytech . . . . +27 (0)31 312 7755

Teds from the Tyne 0191 2621 659

Teeny Bears 02380 446356

THE THING ABOUT BEARS 07769 325932

Threadteds . . . . +31 (0)77 3984960

The Throw Company 01255 475498

Tickety Boo Bears 0774 786 7523

Tin Soldiers Studio . . . . +27 (0)83 305 5954

Toys, Stuffed and Handmade by Susan . . . .
. . . . +1 416 242 6446

Tracie Bears 0330 088 3993

Treasured Teddies 01295 690479

Tweedies 01568 780479

U

Una Casa & Co . . . . +81 (0)6 6170 6579

V

V&A Museum of Childhood 020 898 35200

Valewood Bears 01502 562783

Vectis Auctions 01642 750616

W

Wacky Walker Bears 07851724432

Warrens Bear Patch & MAGICAL REALMS . . . .
. . . . 07803 807584

The Way of the Bear 07889 727087

Wee Beary Tails Bears 01227 741352

Wellhausen & Marquardt Medien +49 (0)404291 77100

Whittle-Le-Woods Bears 01204 706831

The Wild Things . . . . +49 (0)2368 56165

BRITISH TEDDY BEAR FESTIVAL AT WOBURN ABBEY . .
. . . . 07875 874854

Woodland Teddies 01509 267597

Works of Heart . . . . +1 702 448 9519

WMM Publishing Ltd 020 7795 8133

END

International Telephone Information

Dialling the UK from overseas

UK phone numbers in the Guide have been listed with their area dialling code, beginning with a zero. If dialling the UK from overseas please

- begin with your international dialling code
- then dial the UK dialling code – 44
- omit the zero from the start of the area code

Eg 01273 654321 should be dialled as:

Your international dialling code 44 1273 654321

Don't forget to check the time difference of the country you're phoning – to avoid calling in the middle of the night!

Dialling out from the UK – add 00

International phone numbers have been listed beginning with their country dialling code.

From the UK add the international dialling code –00– to the number. Eg +49 (0)987 12345 should be dialled as 00 49 987 12345, omiting the zero in brackets which only applies if within that country. Phone numbers in display advertisements have been included as supplied to us and so may need careful attention to ensure they are dialled correctly; check your phone book or internet for details about phoning abroad. Particularly note differences in ringing & engaged tones.

Europe	GMT + 1 hour	W. Australia	GMT + 7-8 hours	New Zealand	GMT +12 hours
USA & Canada	GMT – 6-8 hours	E. Australia	GMT + 10 hours	Japan	GMT + 9 hours

FESTIVALS

Teddy Bear Trail

The Teddy Bear Trail has been compiled from the entries in our shops and sources sections which we understand to be retail outlets open during normal shop hours. Some are specialist teddy bear shops while others are general toy and gift shops which sell teddy bears. Please check opening times and stock details etc, before travelling a distance. See main listing in the shops section for more information. For your convenience, entries have been grouped into areas (see map below).

The codes which appear after the name of the business refer to the number of makers and different designs which you might expect to find there.

We asked the shops to indicate the bands they fall within. Our questions and the key for the codes appear below.

Question 1:
How many different makers (bear artists or manufacturers) do you normally stock?
A) 1-10   B) 11-25   C) 26-50
D) 51-100   E) over 100

Question 2:
How many different designs/models of teddy bear do you normally have in stock?
F) 1-25   G) 26-100)
H) 101-250   I) over 250

London & Southern Counties

Hampshire	Ibsley	St Martin's Gallery	A/H
Hampshire	Lyndhurst	Paws in the Forest	B/H
Isle of Wight	Ryde	Koko's Bear Shop	B/I
Kent	Cliftonville	Sunny Vintage & Retro &Teddy Hospital	B/G
Kent	Tenterden	Three Bears, The	A/G

London	London	All You Can Bear	B/G
London	London	Hamleys of London	C/I
Surrey	Guildford	Bear Garden, The	D/I
West Sussex	Lindfield	Kieron James Toys	B/F
West Sussex	Steyning	Smiffy Bears	A/G

Central England

Buckinghamshire	Winslow	Brimley Bear Company	A/F
Derbyshire	Ashbourne	Bear Patch, The	C/I
Derbyshire	Bakewell	Bakewell Gift & Bear Shop	B/I
Leicestershire	Coalville	Ashby Bears	B/I
Northants	Kettering	Bear With Me	C/H
Oxfordshire	Farnborough, Banbury	Treasured Teddies	B/H
Oxfordshire	Witney	Teddy Bears of Witney	E/I
Oxfordshire	Henley-on-Thames	Asquiths	E/I
Shropshire	Ironbridge	Bears on the Square	E/I
Staffordshire	Stoke on Trent	One More Bear	C/I
Warwickshire	Coventry	Cejais Bears & Dollshouses	B/I
Warwickshire	Stratford upon Avon	Teddy Bear Shop, The	A/G
Warwickshire	Warwick	Warwick Bears	A/F
West Midlands	Birmingham	Apple Pie House	B/I

The West Country

Cornwall	Padstow	Abbey Bears	B/I
Cornwall	Tintagel	Atique & Urchins Bears	B/I
Devon	Dartmouth	Kingswear Bears and Friends	B/I
Devon	Newton Abbot	Magpies Gifts Ltd	B/I
Dorset	Dorchester	Teddy Bear Museum Shop, The	B/G
Dorset	Lyme Regis	Alice's Bear Shop	D/I
Dorset	Swanage	Brewins' Bruins	C/G
Dorset	Swanage	Corfe Bears	B/I
Somerset	Minehead	Exmoor Teddy Bears	B/I

Eastern Counties

Cambridgeshire	Huntingdon	Bears To Collect	B/I
Essex	Saffron Walden	Abracadabra Teddy Bears	D/I
Essex	Southend	Teddy Station	C/I
Lincolnshire	Lincoln	Stonebow Bears	B/G
Norfolk	Norwich	Bear Shop, The	D/I
Suffolk	Bacton, Stowmarket	Bacton Bears	A/I

The North

West Yorkshire	Halifax	Serendipity	B/H
North Yorkshire	Skipton	Teddy Boutique	B/H
North Yorkshire	York	Shortle, Mary	E/I
South Yorkshire	Sheffield	Bear Emporium, The	C/I
West Yorkshire	Holmfirth	Chocolate Box, The	A/G

Ireland

County Cavan	Bawnboy	Bear Essentials	C/I

When visiting shops please mention you saw them in the UK Teddy Bear Guide 2018

END

Display Advertiser Index

END

To help you feel at home and make the most of your visit to a Hugglets Festival here are some practical tips. You'll probably find them helpful even if it's not your first time.

Those who arrive before the opening time of 10.30am will find a queue winding its way down towards Kensington High Street. Some people arrive very early as they are keen to get the best choice of bears from one or other artist but otherwise the main advantage to arriving much before 10.30am is the free chocolates passed down the line.

If you are coming by car it's possible that the underground car park at the venue will be full by mid-day so the earlier you arrive the better chance there is of getting space (otherwise the alternative is in the nearby Young Street car park but it costs more).

Before joining the queue we recommend you obtain your entry ticket from the Hugglets reception desk at the entrance to the halls. If you already have the correct ticket from the back of the UK Teddy Bear Guide or Festival Programme for example, you can join the queue directly.

Tickets cost £4 on the day for adults or £2 for children – but this issue of the Guide contains two complimentary tickets for each event in 2018.

The queue often gets very long but despite this we usually manage to get everyone in within ten minutes because tickets are already held. If someone in the queue doesn't already have their ticket they just step aside when they get to reception – we sell as fast as possible but a short delay for these ticket buyers is inevitable.

The venue is suitable for wheelchair access (please come directly to reception via the entry point higher up Hornton Street to avoid external stairs). An internal lift is available between the three floors as well as the internal stairs. There are toilet facilities on both the top floor and basement but disabled toilet facilities are limited to the basement.

Before handing in your ticket at the inner door (just past reception) please make sure you complete the prize draw details on the back to stand a chance of winning one of three £50 vouchers to spend at the event.

Winners are announced and invited to collect the voucher from reception. If you need to leave early don't worry – if you win a prize we'll post the voucher to you to spend at the next Hugglets Festival.

If at any time you need to leave the venue and return please ask for a pass-out card at the door as you go out.

Not all exhibitors can take cheque or card payments, especially those from overseas, so it's a good idea to have sufficient cash for your proposed purchases. You may need to visit one of the nearby cash points on Kensington High Street (there are four at the corner of Hornton Street).

If you have coats and bags with you, you can deposit these at the free cloakroom in the basement (hall 3). You can also

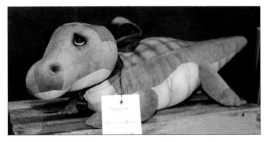

use this facility if your purchases mount up during the day – but don't forget to collect them.

From the point you enter the event everything is open to you – over 10,000 teddy bears and related collectables (sometimes called "soft sculpture" – including rabbits, cats, monkeys, dogs etc) on sale in an enormous variety of styles, sizes, colours, ages and prices.

The event takes place on all three floors and in four different halls:

Ground Floor: Hall 1 - 69 stands
Ground Floor: Hall 2 - 35 stands
Basement: Hall 3 - 36 stands
Top Floor: Hall 4 - 39 stands

Many people find it helpful to review the list of exhibitors before the event. If you've not already received one in the post a floorplan showing exhibitor positions will be available on the day from the reception area. You can collect one when you arrive and review it while waiting in the queue.

You can also use the floorplan in this Guide and obtain the exhibitor list and stand numbers from the Hugglets website. It's a good idea to identify any stands you particularly want to visit early in the day when more bears are still available. But don't forget to look around and allow yourself to discover new things. There are always new exhibitors and young talents worth your attention.

If there are cancellations, additions or changes to the published programme these are posted in various places as you enter the venue.

For about two months prior to a Festival we also provide clickable links on our website to take you to the websites of our exhibitors. This is great for previewing the sorts of bears offered by each exhibitor.

The links remain available on the site for about a year after the event to help you track down an exhibitor if you later regret not buying one of their bears.

If you are especially intent on buying a specific bear or a bear from a particular artist it may be worth contacting the exhibitor in advance in case a bear can be reserved, or perhaps you can buy in advance and collect on the day.

There are so many great bears it will be hard to know where to begin. Most of the leading teddy bear makers in the UK will be there as well as remarkable artists from all over the world.

Hugglets Festivals also offer a rare opportunity to meet bear artists and other exhibitors from overseas - so you'll not want to miss these. There are usually around 60 exhibitors from overseas. They are located through all the halls.

Countries often represented include Australia, Austria, Belgium, Canada, Denmark, Germany, Japan, Norway, Russia, South Africa, Sweden, The Netherlands, Ukraine and USA.

A quick word about photography - if you want to take photos we won't be surprised because the displays are wonderful and the artistry amazing – but please ask permission of the exhibitor first.

Just past the reception area you'll see a bear repairer. You may be lucky to find a repair can be done on the day but often teddies need to become in-patients.

If you are thinking of selling an old bear there are one or two stands who can give valuations for selling at auction. There are also many dealers in old bears who would be pleased to see your bear and perhaps make an offer.

By now you might be getting hungry, so on the top floor you'll find the snack bar. An alternative is to take a break outside at one the local eateries or find a seat in the balcony area overlooking Hall One and break out the sandwiches! If you do go out for food please note that fast food cannot be brought back into the premises so you'll need to finish it outside.

If you are coming with a party it is a good idea to arrange a meeting time and place in case you split up. Sorry, we generally won't make public announcements to reunite you with your friends, but we make an exception if children are lost.

On the subject of things being lost, please keep hold of your bags. You'll need to put them down to cuddle an irresistible bear from time to time but remember to pick them up again. If you do lose something please report it to the Hugglets reception at the entrance.

We'll take your contact details and reunite you with your property if it is handed in. If you find something, please bring it to reception and if it is next to a stand please also bring it to the attention of the exhibitor.

In case you feel unwell during the event (overwhelmed by all the bears?) there are two St John Ambulance staff on site to help you – please ask at reception.

The event finishes at 4.00pm so you'll want to regroup and make sure you've visited all the halls before then. At 3.45pm we make an announcement to recommend you make your final purchases before the journey home. If you have left items in the cloakroom please collect them. Anything still there at the end of the day will be transferred to the Hugglets reception desk.

If you are hoping to get a taxi we advise you to walk down to the main road and hail one from there. Phoning for a cab is not always successful.

If you have parked in the car park, you'll need to pay at the machine or at the manned booth before rejoining your car. Payment is only accepted by card.

Have a safe journey back and we hope your adopted bears settle well into their new home.

If you think other things should be added to this page please let us know by emailing contact@hugglets.co.uk

We are looking forward to welcoming you in Kensington Town Hall.

Sebastian Marquardt
and the Hugglets Team

How to exhibit with Hugglets

Although most space is allocated to our long standing exhibitors we can always allocate some spaces at each event to exhibitors who are new to Hugglets. You are welcome to register your interest at any time by supplying a few pictures of your work (this can be done most easily by email attachment) and an indication of which events you are interested in attending.

When we receive your "registration of interest" we will acknowledge receipt and if we feel we might be able to offer space at some point in the future, we will keep your photographs on file for consideration whenever space comes up. Stands are generally allocated to newcomers about six months prior to each event though there are also usually a few late cancellations.

Due to the large number of applicants we do not operate a purely time-based waiting list. Our assessment is based on the originality and quality of work and overall appeal as perceived from your photos. We will also note recommendations from existing exhibitors. Since 2003 we have been implementing a points system which also takes note of advertising in the UK Teddy Bear Guide (visitors are often keen to see exhibitors they recognise from the Guide).

Not all exhibitors are bear artists. We also include specialist bear shops, dealers in old bears and suppliers of other related products and services such as bear-making supplies.

Hugglets Teddy Bear Festivals take place in February and September. The tables are generally 183cm long by 76cm wide (6' x 2' 6") though some are wider. Prices vary from £150 to £195 plus VAT. Our general policy is to make only single stands available in order to include as many applicants as possible (a few exhibitors do have two stands for historical reasons). Future dates and further details are available on our website at www.hugglets.co.uk

Offers to exhibitors who are new to our events are often on a "one-off" basis to start with because often the stands are only available temporarily. (For clarification, this doesn't mean you won't be invited again if you are unable to accept our offer of stand space. Nor does it mean that you can only come once and then won't be invited back.)

You can email or write your request to be on the waiting list (don't forget to include some pictures or point us to your website).

We look forward to hearing from you! contact@hugglets.co.uk

FESTIVALS Hugglets

Your complimentary tickets are on pages 139-142

Please see overleaf for floorplans

For exhibitor lists & visitor information please see

www.hugglets.co.uk

Venue – Kensington Town Hall Hornton Street, London, W8 7NX.

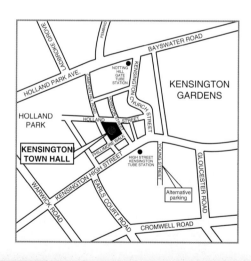

Entry times

10.30am - 4.00pm
Tickets at door:
£4 for adults,
£2 for children.

Parking under venue costs £10
for 9am-6pm.
400 spaces.
Nearest Tube is
High Street Kensington

WMM Publishing Ltd
St James House, 13 Kensington Square
London W8 5HD, United Kingdom

Phone: +44(0)20-77 95 81 33
Email: contact@hugglets.co.uk
Internet: www.hugglets.co.uk

Hugglets Festivals Floorplans

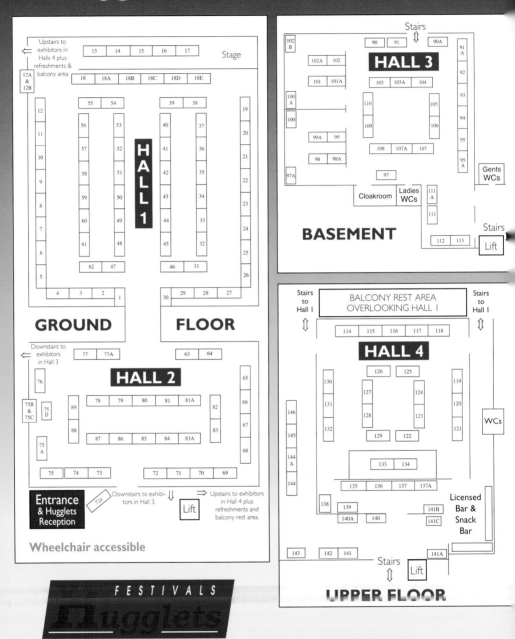

GROUND FLOOR

HALL 1

Upstairs to exhibitors in Halls 4 plus refreshments & balcony area

| 13 | 14 | 15 | 16 | 17 | Stage |

12A & 12B | 18 | 18A | 18B | 18C | 18D | 18E

55 54 · 39 38 · 12 · 19
56 53 · 40 37 · 11 · 20
57 52 · 41 36 · 10 · 21
58 51 · 42 35 · 9 · 22
59 50 · 43 34 · 8 · 23
60 49 · 44 33 · 7 · 24
61 48 · 45 32 · 6 · 25
62 47 · 46 31 · 5 · 26
4 3 2 1 · 30 · 29 28 27

HALL 2

Downstairs to exhibitors in Hall 3

77 77A · 63 64
76 · 65
75B & 75C · 75D · 89 · 78 79 80 81 81A · 82 · 66
88 · 83 · 67
75A · 87 86 85 84 83A · 68
75 74 73 · 72 71 70 69

Entrance & Hugglets Reception

Downstairs to exhibitors in Hall 3. Lift Upstairs to exhibitors in Hall 4 plus refreshments and balcony rest area.

Wheelchair accessible

BASEMENT

HALL 3

Stairs

102B · 90 91 · 90A · 91A
102A 102 · 92
101 101A · 103 103A 104 · 93
100A · 110 · 105 · 94
100 · 109 · 106 · 95
99A 99 · 108 107A 107 · 95A
98 98A · Gents WCs
97A · 97 · 111A
Cloakroom · Ladies WCs · 111
Stairs
112 113 · Lift

UPPER FLOOR

HALL 4

Stairs to Hall 1 · BALCONY REST AREA OVERLOOKING HALL 1 · Stairs to Hall 1

114 115 116 117 118

130 · 126 125 · 119
131 · 127 124 · 120
146 · 128 123 · WCs
145 · 132 · 129 122 · 121
144A · 133 134
144 · 135 136 137 137A
138 · 139 · 141B · Licensed Bar & Snack Bar
140A 140 · 141C
143 142 141 · 141A
Stairs Lift

For exhibitor lists: www.hugglets.co.uk

138   *Hugglets Festivals Information*

WINTER BEARFEST

Valid for adult or child entry from 10.30am – 4.00pm

25th February 2018

Kensington Town Hall, Hornton St., London W8 7NX
Extra tickets on sale at reception

Please enter the prize draw on the reverse of this ticket

Come to the Winter BearFest

... and bring a friend!

Please enter the prize draw on the reverse of this ticket

WINTER BEARFEST

Valid for adult or child entry from 10.30am – 4.00pm

25th February 2018

Kensington Town Hall, Hornton St., London W8 7NX
Extra tickets on sale at reception

Prize Draw – you could win £50!

Before handing in your ticket please complete details for your chance to win one of four £50 vouchers to spend at a Hugglets Festival. First draw at 12, then hourly. You will be entered into all draws. Limited to one entry per person. Unclaimed winners will be notified by mail.

Please enter clearly:

Name ....

Address ....

Town ....

County ....

Postcode ....

Email (if any) ....

Prize Draw – you could win £50!

Before handing in your ticket please complete details for your chance to win one of four £50 vouchers to spend at a Hugglets Festival. First draw at 12, then hourly. You will be entered into all draws. Limited to one entry per person. Unclaimed winners will be notified by mail.

Please enter clearly:

Name ....

Address ....

Town ....

County ....

Postcode ....

Email (if any) ....

TEDDIES FESTIVAL

IN SEPTEMBER

Valid for adult or child entry
from 10.30am – 4.00pm

9th September 2018

**Kensington Town Hall, Hornton St., London W8 7NX
Extra tickets on sale at reception**

Please enter the prize draw on the reverse of this ticket

Come to Teddies 2018

... and bring a friend!

Please enter the prize draw on the reverse of this ticket

TEDDIES FESTIVAL

IN SEPTEMBER

Valid for adult or child entry
from 10.30am – 4.00pm

9th September 2018

**Kensington Town Hall, Hornton St., London W8 7NX
Extra tickets on sale at reception**

Prize Draw – you could win £50!

Before handing in your ticket please complete details for your chance to win one of four £50 vouchers to spend at a Hugglets Festival. First draw at 12, then hourly. You will be entered into all draws. Limited to one entry per person. Unclaimed winners will be notified by mail.

Please enter clearly:

Name ....

Address ....

Town ....

County ....

Postcode ....

Email (if any) ....

Prize Draw – you could win £50!

Before handing in your ticket please complete details for your chance to win one of four £50 vouchers to spend at a Hugglets Festival. First draw at 12, then hourly. You will be entered into all draws. Limited to one entry per person. Unclaimed winners will be notified by mail.

Please enter clearly:

Name ....

Address ....

Town ....

County ....

Postcode ....

Email (if any) ....